A BURRO FOR JESUS
One man's adventures with God

Burro sketch by Kelly Shehan Hazime

My life is worth nothing to me unless I use it for finishing the work assigned me by _____ ___ ___ ___ work of telling others the Good News ab_____ (Acts 20:24)

D1533948

Sunrise Solutions, LLC

Endorsements

I quote from chapter 4 – "Next time God asks you to do something – say yes. If it doesn't seem logical – say yes anyway. If you seem unqualified – God isn't. Say yes." Read the rest of this in Chapter 4. This is a phrase that characterizes my good friend Bert Hunt. I believe you will be challenged and inspired to say – YES – after reading *"A Burro For Jesus"*.
Gary Olander, *member of Cru (formerly Campus Crusade for Christ)*

❦❦❦❦❦❦❦❦❦❦❦❦❦❦❦❦❦❦

I see Bert Hunt often around town and our church sitting one on one with someone. Regardless of who they are, I always pass by thinking, "There's another person God is going to change and bless through Bert." But Bert is not such a treasure because of his one-of-a-kind talent or top-notch education. Bert is a treasure because he is faithful to the One who treasures him. He is an ordinary person like any of us who has simply said yes to Jesus' call on his life. This book is his story to that end. *A Burro For Jesus* is an important book for many reasons. It covers the issues of Jesus' love for all people, matters of prayer and family, identifying people in need, and how to grow in being used by God for amazing things. In all this, Bert puts matters on the bottom shelf for all of us to access. You'll see yourself in Bert and the countless cast of characters that have come across his path and onto the pages of this book. God has been using Bert to change one life a time for years now. Read this book and be another life changed by Jesus.
Ron Merrell, *Lead Pastor of The Heights Church*

❦❦❦❦❦❦❦❦❦❦❦❦❦❦❦❦❦❦

Do we hurt for the lost? Jesus' heart is for them. As Bert Hunt takes us on his journey of truly "loving them like Jesus", he brings all the glory to God and seeks to disciple as Jesus commands all of us.
Norman Cheever
Az. Director, Full Gospel Business Men's Fellowship International

🔺 A BURRO FOR JESUS

Bert Hunt is an ordinary man who has done extraordinary things through the power of the Holy Spirit. I have known Bert for many years and have witnessed how God has used him to push forward the Kingdom agenda of love, mercy, and grace. You will be inspired and challenged by Bert's simple stories of ministry as he walks surrendered to the purposes of God in his life.
Brad Small, *President of Embark Ministries*

❦❦❦❦❦❦❦❦❦❦❦❦❦❦❦❦

I thank God that He brought Bert Hunt into my life and our church over 20 years ago. As his pastor and friend, I have marveled at his consistent sensitivity to the leading of the Spirit, his willingness to follow wherever that leads and how God shows up in the process. In some ways, I am surprised that Bert has written this book. He is the consummate servant who works behind the scene and who avoids drawing attention to himself. On the other hand, it makes perfect sense for him to record some of his experiences in walking with the Lord for it is Bert's greatest joy to tell others how wonderful Jesus is. He seeks to convey this message through his actions and his words. I can attest that the events recorded in this book are true and accurate, that Bert's love for Jesus is deep and genuine and that his compassion for people – especially people who are in need – is undeniable and palpable. The Lord has used Bert to enrich my life and to encourage me to increasingly live by faith and not by sight. I pray that He will do the same for you as you join Bert in his journey with Jesus.
Dr. Rick Efird, *Desert Springs Bible Church, Phoenix Seminary*

A BURRO FOR JESUS

Introduction

After you read this book, you may forget my name. That's OK. But I hope you remember the title *"A Burro for Jesus"*.

What's the significance of the burro? Remember when Jesus rode the donkey (burro) into Jerusalem? The people there cheered and praised Jesus because of who He was and all He had done. (Matthew, chapter 21, in the Bible). As far as we know, this was an ordinary donkey until Jesus got on his back and rode him into the city. There's no indication that he was an unusually talented donkey, but he became part of this very special event because Jesus decided to use him. I imagine he was just an ordinary donkey again when Jesus dismounted him. How silly it would have been if the donkey had gone home bragging about how much he did for Jesus that day and how people had cheered for both of them. It's not important that we know the name of the donkey (if he had one). It's only important that he was available to be used by Jesus and that Jesus received the praise and honor.

I'm just like that donkey. I'm very ordinary. But when I allow Jesus to use me, I see Him do amazing things. When I choose to try things on my own, I'm ordinary again. I've had the privilege of watching God do remarkable things over the years through me and through others. It's not important if people remember any of our names. However, it's very important that we continue to make ourselves available for Jesus to use and that He receives the praise and honor He deserves.

Many years ago, I was an atheist. I didn't believe in God at all. My life was all about me. When I discovered that God was real, I found a life with Him that was (and is) better than anything I'd ever known before. It was an exciting time – experiencing the goodness of God and learning more about His plan for me. My life had a new purpose, it had real meaning. In Jesus, I had a new best friend – one who would never let me down.

God, in all of His goodness, changed everything in my life. As I began to focus more on Him and my love for Him deepened, my life became an all-consuming explosion of His joy and His love. As the love I felt from Him began to naturally flow from me to the people I met, I saw their lives impacted by God's love. My life became an adventure with God – as I enjoyed Him and took His love and peace to people who were hurting and in need of Him.

Although I'm mentioned in the stories that follow, this book is not about me. It's about how God changed my life and used me to change my small part of the world – one life at a time. It's about what happens when a powerful, loving God chooses to do His work through an average person like me (just like that burro). These stories are true. As often as possible, I have verified the facts with others who were there with me. When unsure of the exact details, I have tried to understate the facts and never exaggerate. My God is powerful and wonderful. His actions speak for themselves and need not be embellished.

Please join me as I tell you about my adventures with God . . .

Published by Sunrise Solutions, LLC
Visit: www.h10ministries.com or
A Burro for Jesus- Facebook page
Prescott, AZ.

Printed in the United States of America

A Burro for Jesus,
One man's adventures with God

Cover photo: istockart.com
Cover and back cover design by Glenda Johnson

Unless otherwise indicated all scripture quotations are taken from the New Living Bible Translation

Although the stories in this book are true, some of the names have been changed because it was difficult or impossible to get permission to use their name and because some of the people asked that their name not be used so the focus would be on Jesus, not on them.

ISBN #-13: 9781542803503
ISBN #-10: 154289350X

 A BURRO FOR JESUS

ACKNOWLEDGEMENTS

THANK YOU . . .

JESUS
Everything good I have in my life is because of you.

Stephanie, James, Kristy, Stephen, Kelley, Jennifer, Mason, Payton, Logan, Mylie, Jackson
My wife and family – how you enrich my life.

Diana
For suggesting I write this book.

Sandra, Jennifer
For many hours editing and navigating through these stories.
I see your handprints all over this book.

Kelly, Glenda, Debra, Cheri
Your additional editing, illustrations and design work
have been invaluable as this book came together.

Jesus
I mention you again …
because I like saying your name and seeing it in print –
You are the best!

A BURRO FOR JESUS

CONTENTS

CONTENTS

The
Adventure
Begins

Chapter 1

The Journey

Trust in the Lord with all your heart; do not depend on your own understanding. Seek His will in all you do, and He will show you which path to take. Proverbs 3:5-6

Before I tell you about my adventures with God, let me tell you briefly about my prior life. My childhood memories are happy ones. I had loving parents and a very good family life. But for most of my early years, God was not a meaningful part of my life. Although my parents took us to church often when I was young, it meant very little to me at the time. Going to church seemed to be something we did because it was Sunday. I don't remember God's name ever being mentioned in our home. I don't remember us reading the Bible together or praying together as a family (except for a prayer that was recited without much meaning before meals). God seemed to be an abstract concept that had no relevance to my daily life.

While in high school, I became convinced by one of my teachers that God didn't exist. **That's when I became an atheist.** I was convinced that all the stories about God that I had heard in church were either made up or exaggerated. I thought they were only believed by people who were weak, not strong enough to make it on their own without some silly superstition to rely upon. I really bought into the world's philosophy . . . that it's all about me . . . that we only go around once during this life, so we have to be strong and independent and get as much as we can because this is all there is. With this philosophy being practiced by so many people, it's no wonder the world is in such chaos.

Then, when I was in my junior year of high school, a few of

my friends invited me to their church. I went and I heard a man speak about Jesus wanting to be my best friend. For the first time in my life, I understood that Jesus is alive today; that He loved me and He had a purpose for my life. He wanted me to believe in Him and follow Him. Somehow, I knew it was true. **So I became a believer in Jesus.**

The next year I met and fell in love with Stephanie – the most beautiful, most wonderful girl in the world. We knew almost immediately that we wanted to spend the rest of our lives together. 3 years later we became husband and wife. We've now been happily married for 41 years and God has blessed us with 3 children, 2 daughters-in-law and 5 grandchildren. It was a wonderful time as Stephanie and I began our married life together and shared our walk with Jesus together.

But gradually, over time, I allowed my life to get busy with other things (family, career, hobbies, etc.). These things weren't bad, but as I became more focused on them and less focused on God, my life as a Christian became somewhat casual. I was comfortable in my American lifestyle and also comfortable in my Christian life. I had been doing life the way I had been taught – finish high school and college, go to church, get married, work hard, have children, etc. I knew God cared about all aspects of my life because He cared about me and wanted me to be happy. But I hadn't yet learned that our lives are better when we love God above all things and ask Him to lead us in every part of our lives. I thought I was doing things the right way, but I wasn't. I worked hard for God when I was serving in the church, then I worked hard for me the rest of the week. I wanted God's best in my life but I didn't want to give Him my best. I thought I could love and pursue God AND the things of this world at the same time – and get the best of both . . .

I was wrong. Something was missing in my walk with God. I wanted to experience more of Him. Then …

A BURRO FOR JESUS

When I was about 45 years old, something happened while on my journey with God. It began when He created in me a hunger for Him that I couldn't satisfy and I began to read the Bible and pray more often. As I became more obsessed with Him and my love for Him deepened, everything became better – the relationships in my life, my marriage, my work, my spiritual journey – everything!

During this time, there were three very memorable events in my life. The first event was very unusual and happened while I was driving out of town on a business trip. It was about 6 o'clock in the morning and I was driving on a winding mountain road in the dark while listening to a Christian music CD. All of a sudden, the presence of God became so real inside my car that I felt like I could cut it with a knife. I had never experienced anything like this before, but somehow I knew it was real and it was from God. My mind became flooded with thoughts that I knew were coming from Him – thoughts about how much He loved me. I was totally absorbed by what was happening. It was completely overwhelming yet very peaceful.

As strange as it may sound as I describe it now, it didn't seem unusual while it was happening. I didn't want to forget any of the thoughts that were dominating my mind, so I reached for a pen and paper and began writing them down as I was driving. After a few minutes I realized I was weaving in and out of my lane on that mountain road as I was writing.

I thought, "If I don't pull off the road, I'm going to hit an oncoming car or go over the side of this mountain. If I don't pull over, I'm going to kill myself or someone else."

So, I parked on the side of the road and for about 45 minutes continued to write down the thoughts that were coming rapidly from God. It still seemed that my car was so filled with His presence that I could almost touch Him. I don't know exactly what happened on that mountain road or why God chose to give this message to me. But as I look back on it now, God was beginning to change the direction of my life.

The second event that happened wasn't as dramatic, but it was just as meaningful to me. As I was driving home from an out-of-town business trip, I sensed in my mind a very specific thought that I thought must be coming from God.

I felt like God was telling me, "If you devote the rest of your life, your time and your resources to Me and to telling others about Me, and only one person comes to know Jesus personally, it'll be worth it. **Every single life is important to Me.**"

I remember thinking, "I don't want to limp into heaven by myself. I want to take others with me."

The third event is described in more detail in Chapter 3, "The Coat." I began to wonder if God wanted me to quit my job and begin serving Him full-time in some way. Then I got a definite impression from God, as if He was telling me, "You don't have to quit your job to serve Me. Just be faithful where I've put you. You have neighbors and friends who don't know Me yet."

God was telling me that where we live now is our mission field, full of people looking for answers in life … answers that can only be found in Him. He was telling me that He has given us a wonderful purpose in life – to know Him personally and to make Him and his love known to the people we meet.

As I offered my life to God for His use . . . I watched as He used me to take His love to people who needed a touch from Him. It was then that my journey with Him truly became an adventure.

🌾🌾🌾🌾🌾🌾🌾🌾🌾🌾🌾🌾🌾🌾🌾

Dear reader, I encourage you to seek God's plan for your life, and discover the joy of following Jesus!

Chapter 2

Rick

I bring my requests to You and wait expectantly. Psalm 5:3

Many years ago, before the three events mentioned at the end of the last chapter, my wife and I moved our family to Arizona. We joined a church as soon as we arrived there, but somehow it didn't seem to be all that we wanted in a church. Over time, we began to skip church and sleep in on Sundays. One day while I was at work, I realized we hadn't been to church in months. So I came up with an idea. I went around the office making a list of the churches everyone attended, determined to attend each one until I found a new church.

Then the thought occurred to me, "How stupid of me. I have this list of churches but I haven't prayed about it yet. God knows where He wants us to go to church; I should ask Him."

So, I put the list away and prayed. I asked God to lead us to the church He wanted for us. This all happened late Friday afternoon. The next morning, my doorbell rang. There was a man at the door I didn't know. He said his name was Rick and that he was the pastor of a local neighborhood church. People from his church were going door-to-door in my neighborhood that day giving out a film about Jesus.

As Pastor Rick told me about his church that Saturday morning, it seemed to be exactly what we were looking for. It had been right down the street from us this whole time, but I had never noticed it before. So, the next morning we went to Pastor Rick's church for the first time.

I discovered years later that one of the men in the church had been "prayer walking" in our area for months. His name is Gary. He walked the streets in our neighborhood (including my cul-de-sac) praying that the people in each house would be receptive to his church's efforts on that Saturday.

This became our church for about 20 years until my wife and I moved to a new city. Rick was my pastor for all of those years. Gary has become a dear friend. God has used Rick, Gary and others in that church to impact my life in more ways than I can count.

I'm so glad for all those days that Gary walked by my house and prayed for me and my family. I'm so glad I put my list away that Friday afternoon and prayed.

🌱🌱🌱🌱🌱🌱🌱🌱🌱🌱🌱🌱🌱🌱🌱

How much better things are when we look to God for answers. So let's pray often with a sincere heart, seeking His direction in every decision we make – big or small.

Prayer works!

A BURRO FOR JESUS

Chapter 3

The Coat

If someone has enough money to live well and sees a brother or sister in need but shows no compassion – how can God's love be in that person? 1 John 3:17

One Christmas morning, I was surprised as I opened the gifts from my wife and realized I was getting one coat after another. She knew that I would sometimes give my coat to a homeless person who didn't have one, then she would buy me another new coat. That year, she bought me three coats and half-jokingly asked me to try to keep one of them for myself (thank you, Lord, for a wife with a generous, giving heart). I really did intend to keep one for myself, but it didn't work out that way.

A month or so later, I was driving home from a business trip late at night. I was tired and still had more than one hour of driving ahead of me. I was going to grab some drive-thru fast food to eat as I continued driving home, but changed my mind at the last minute. **I wanted to read my Bible while I ate dinner, so I went inside.**

Once inside, I heard one of the employees mention God's name several times. I was reading at the time and wasn't listening closely to her. I didn't realize until later that she had used God's name as profanity. She was a small woman and older than most people I usually see working in a fast food hamburger restaurant.

When she came near my table I said, "Hi. I heard you mention God's name. He's been my best friend for a long time. Do you know Him too?"

I was surprised by her answer.

She said, "There is no God. If there was a God, my life wouldn't be so hard right now."

"I'm sorry." I said, "Would you like to talk about it?"

She immediately sat down at my table and began to tell me about the difficulties in her life. **She seemed to have no hope.** I told her about my God and His love for her. As we talked, I glanced at her manager from time to time. I didn't want her to get into trouble for sitting at my table for so long, but the manager didn't seem to mind. We talked for about ten minutes, and then I asked if I could pray for her. When she said yes, I asked God to help her with her current problems and to help her find the peace and the hope that comes only from Him.

As I got up to leave, I asked her if she could come outside with me while I looked in my car for a book I thought she would enjoy. I carry books and Bibles with me just for this reason. People joke about the "library" in my car, but I think everyone should carry Christian books and Bibles and sleeping bags in their car. You never know when you'll meet someone who needs one. I don't mind that my car is overloaded and cluttered sometimes, or that I often have to clear off one of the seats when I give someone a ride!

It was cold outside as we stood and talked for a few minutes. After I gave her the book and a Bible, I noticed that she wasn't wearing a coat, so I asked her if she had a good winter coat. When she said no, my first thought was that I should give her the one I was wearing. I hesitated for a moment, because I had told my wife I'd try to keep one of the coats for myself, and I had already given the other two away. Fortunately, my hesitation was brief. The coat was meant for my new friend – not for me.

As I got into my car, I watched her move slowly as she headed back inside. She was slightly bent over as she walked. She seemed so small and frail. I knew she may still be burdened by her circumstances and may not have been completely convinced about God's love for her. I was glad I could give her a brief glimpse at God's goodness through my words and through the warm coat, book and Bible. I was comforted by the thought that God would send someone else to tell her about the peace she could find in Him, because that's what He does. I was reminded again that we often don't see immediate results when we try to love people for God and lead them to Jesus. But none of this is about us seeing results. It's not about us at all. **It's all about loving people for God because He first loved us and asks us to love others.**

The world doesn't seem to have much concern for people like this small, broken woman I met that night. But God does. How good it was to know that God arranged this meeting to remind her that He's a God of comfort and that she's not alone. As I drove away, I felt that God was telling me that this is what He wanted my life to be about – telling others about His wonderful love for them – with both actions and words.

❦❦❦❦❦❦❦❦❦❦❦❦❦❦❦❦❦❦

**Let's slow down and listen to the people around us –
God can use these moments to touch others.**

Being a Burro for Jesus
In Mexico

Chapter 4

Say Yes

Then I heard the Lord asking,
"Whom should I send as a messenger to this people?
Who will go for us?" I said, "Here I am. Send me."
Isaiah 6:8

A short time after the incident with the coat mentioned in the last chapter, my daughter and I joined people from our church for a weekend mission trip to Mexico. I expected to go and do some nice things to help the people there but I didn't expect to be so affected by the trip. **I was overwhelmed by the poverty I saw.** I had no way of knowing at the time how God would use this and subsequent trips to Mexico to impact the rest of my life.

I was very impressed by Jay and Rose, the husband and wife team from Arizona who led weekend trips to Mexico every month. They had such a commitment to ministering to the poor there. I was so inspired by their example, that I called them after we returned from the trip and told them that I wanted to do more to help them minister to the people in Mexico. So, I began to join them on all of their monthly trips.

One winter day, while standing on a street in Mexico, Rose told me about several children who had died there recently. They lived like most people did in that area – in small shacks with no electricity and no running water. Many of these shacks were built on the sand and were made out of any scraps of wood or plastic or paper they could find. During a recent rainstorm, a lot of the families who lived inside these shacks got wet because their roofs leaked. As a result of this and the lack of heat inside the houses, some of the children caught colds. Their colds turned into pneumonia then tragically, several children died because their families didn't have enough money to buy the medicine needed to help their children. Being a parent, I couldn't imagine the anguish of watching your children slowly die and not being able to help them.

I was heartbroken. When it rains in the US, we can go inside our homes and we don't get wet. If we get sick, we have medicine available to us. But in Mexico, there were families burying their children just because they were poor and their housing was so inadequate.

After I returned home from the weekend trip, I couldn't stop thinking about the children who died. Although I knew nothing about construction, I felt strongly that we had to do something to help the housing situation in this part of Mexico. So within a few weeks, Rose and I went back to Mexico to meet with Pastor Carlos, a local pastor in the community where the children had recently died. We asked if he would introduce us to families who needed a new roof on their house; then we all drove around as he took us to several tiny houses.

At the first house we met a very nice family of four who actually lived in a house built out of pieces of cardboard. Then we went to Angelina's house. Like the other houses in the area, it was built on sand. It was really just one big room with its outer walls made out of drywall. Once inside, I saw three pieces of furniture (2 beds and a dresser) that almost filled up the entire house. To go from one side of the room to the other, you actually had to crawl across the two beds. The inside of their little house was so neat that even the small area of sand floor had been swept smooth with a broom. Angelina had several adorable children, two of whom had disabilities. Jorge had a condition that affected his eyesight and little Maria had been born with club feet.

After visiting with six families, we told Pastor Carlos that our group would return soon to repair roofs that leaked. Then he pointed out a fact I had overlooked; we were planning to build a new roof on a shack that might fall down next time there was a big storm. He suggested we build new houses for the people, not just replace existing roofs. Of course he was right; I hadn't thought of that! **So we decided that the ministry in Mexico would now include building houses!**

A few weeks later, my son and I went to California to speak with a friend who was the director of a large ministry that built homes for the poor in Mexico. He told us how they organized trips to Mexico to build new homes and he gave us a copy of the floor plan they used. Shortly thereafter, I spoke with the pastor of my church. With his approval, we announced to our congregation that we would go down to Mexico soon to begin building houses for some of the families who lived in these shacks. Very quickly we had a group of about 20 people who wanted to join us to build the first house . . . How exciting!

About a month or so before the trip, my daughter came to me one morning and said, "Dad, you know we're going to Mexico soon to build a house."

"I know. Isn't that exciting?"

"You know, none of us know how to build a house."

"I know."

"You know, we don't have the money to buy the lumber."

"I know."

"So . . . what's the plan?" she asked jokingly, but with a note of sincerity.

"We're going to pray. That's the plan. We know God wants us to do this, so let's ask Him to take care of the details. He knows someone who can provide the lumber and someone who knows how to build a house. We just need Him to tell us who they are."

So we prayed and asked God for what we needed. Within

several days, my daughter came home from college excited about what had happened that day.

She said, "I met a girl at school today. Her dad works for a construction company. His name is Rudy. She thinks he may want to help us. She gave me his phone number."

I called Rudy and we scheduled a time to meet to talk about the trip to Mexico. Within a week or so, four other men who worked in the construction industry heard about the project and said they wanted to help. Without any announcements or emails asking for help, God provided a team of talented men to help with the first house!

I invited the men over to my house and listened as we sat around my kitchen table and discussed the upcoming project, but it made very little sense to me because I knew almost nothing about building a house. After considering the California floor plan, the men came up with a design that was similar but slightly different.

It would be a small house by our standards (12' x 28') and only have two rooms. There would be no electrical wires or plumbing because the neighborhood in Mexico had no running water or electricity. **It was really just a small framed structure, but to a family living in a shack, it would be something of great value.** It was big by their standards and it would be built on concrete with a roof that wouldn't leak. They would stay warm and dry in the winter.

As the six of us continued to talk, someone asked if we were buying the lumber in Mexico or here in the U.S. I said I wasn't sure yet. I told them that it would cost less here, but I didn't have a truck to transport the lumber to Mexico. I also told them that we had almost no money for the materials needed, but we expected God to provide it before the trip. I mentioned this as a matter of information. I didn't expect them to donate anything except their time and expertise to this project.

Then, one of the men in the group said, "I'll donate the lumber." Another said, "I'll donate the truck and trailer."

As expected, God provided the experienced men and the materials to build our first house! We had already decided before this meeting to do one small fund-raising event. At the time, it seemed like a logical way to get the money we needed. It turned out to be a fun evening, but we only raised about $200. After that, I decided to do no more fund-raising for the rest of the Mexico construction projects. We didn't send out e-mails or letters asking for money. We had no regular source of funding. We didn't ask our church to budget money for the building of houses on future mission trips. We decided to rely upon prayer for direction and provision, expecting God to do what He does – supply what is needed for the work He wants done.

As I look back on those 4 ½ years of ministry, our decision to rely entirely on prayer for what we needed wasn't a conscious effort to be "super spiritual". I actually don't remember giving it a lot of thought. It just seemed natural – God was leading us so He would provide. That's who He is – He's our God and our friend who never lets us down. Although there is nothing wrong with having an organized fund-raising strategy, I felt it made more sense for us to devote our efforts to listening to God for direction, and then do what we felt He wanted us to do.

We became accustomed, over the years, to Him directing us to build a house for someone. Then we would start planning for the house-building trip although we didn't have the money or the materials at the time. We were never surprised when God provided what we needed (often at the last minute), but we were very aware of His continual faithfulness. After all, what leader sends out his troops without providing for their needs?

And how God provided over the next few years! How we saw lives touched in Mexico through the ministry! How our lives were touched! For more than 4 ½ years we went to Mexico at least once every month. Rudy led the construction of each new house (except twice when he couldn't join us). Hundreds of people joined the effort and gave their time, their talents, their money and their hearts to these trips. During these years, we built 22 houses (for families or ministries in Mexico) and repaired another 10 homes. We passed out more clothes, medicine, toys, Bibles and eyeglasses than we could count. We also helped distribute tons of food (literally tons) to the hungry, as a part of Jay and Rose's ongoing ministry.

By the way, before that first year was over, we built two houses – one for each of the 2 families mentioned earlier (the family living in the cardboard house and for Angelina's family). We stayed very close to Angelina's family during the following years.

A little while after we built her new house, we brought her and her daughter Maria to the USA to try to find someone to do the surgery needed for Maria's club feet. While on that trip to the States, several of us were sitting with Angelina and her 1 year old daughter when Maria took her first steps. Because her club feet were turned completely in and under, she actually walked on her ankles. But she didn't know the difference. She took about ten steps with no help and had the most beautiful smile on her face. It was quite a moment. Before we could make arrangements for the surgery, Angelina found a way to have the surgery done in Mexico. It was a complete success.

Toward the end of that year, Angelina told Pastor Carlos, "This has been a wonderful year for my family. We got a new house, my baby had an operation for her feet and my husband and I became Christians. The best part of the year was that we became Christians."

Within the next two years, Angelina also found a way for Jorge to have the surgery needed to correct his eyes. It seemed like these two children were at almost every children's activity we conducted in Mexico for years. They were such happy kids. It was always a joy to see them running and playing with the other children – with their disabilities being a thing of the past.

During the years of ministry in Mexico, I was often surprised that my God chose me (with no experience in mission work or construction) to help Jay and Rose in their ministry. My primary role was to organize and lead people from my church who joined the monthly mission trips and to help plan and organize the house building endeavors, with the help of many talented people who God brought into the ministry.

God told me and others to go...So we did.
He asked us to trust Him...So we did.
He did the rest!

ꕥꕥꕥꕥꕥꕥꕥꕥꕥꕥꕥꕥꕥꕥ

Next time God asks you to do something – say yes.
If it doesn't seem logical - say yes anyway.
If you seem unqualified - God isn't - say yes anyway.
God honors obedience . . .
Obedience is a reflection of our love
for Him and our trust in Him.

Chapter 5

God Has a Reason

"I know that You can do all things;
no purpose of Yours can be thwarted.
Job 42:2 (NIV)

In 2004, after several months of planning, our group went to Mexico to build the first of many houses for people who lived in tiny shacks. From the start, the trip from our church to the Mexican border was full of surprises. We never expected to have so much trouble crossing the border. We also didn't expect God to use one of the young men in our group (Nate) the way He did to help get us across the border. Nate really loves God a lot. He is a talented musician and has a big heart for serving others.

We had a plan for the trip to Mexico. God had a better plan. The truck and the trailer had been loaded the night before with the lumber and tools we needed to build the house. Our plan was for Nate to come over to my house at 6:00 a.m. to help me load the furniture that had been donated as a "house-warming" gift for the family in Mexico. We would then join our group at the church and drive to Mexico. We expected to arrive at the border at about 10:00 a.m.

But, from the start, things didn't go according to plan. Nate overslept and arrived at my house at about 6:30 a.m., not 6:00. Then, we had to make a trip to the lumber store to pick up materials for another ministry in Mexico. They heard that I was planning to go to Mexico, so they called me the night before and asked me to pick up some lumber for them. When Nate and I finally arrived at the church to join the rest of our group, we were already about two hours behind schedule.

But none of us cared. **A little delay was not going to lessen the excitement we all felt.** We discussed a few details about the trip and then prayed as a group.

As we were getting into our cars and trucks to leave, there was a problem. Nate had accidentally locked his keys in his car, so we all waited while someone took him home to get a spare set of keys and return to the church.

We still didn't care about this further delay. We were excited to be on our way to Mexico to bless a family there with a new house.

Finally we were off!

When we were about one hour from the border, I noticed that one of the cars in our caravan was missing. It was Jay's red van. Jay had volunteered to be the "caboose" (the last vehicle in our caravan). I asked for a volunteer to drive back and see if Jay was stranded on the side of the road with car trouble, while the rest of us waited where we were by the side of the road until both vehicles rejoined our group. Guess who volunteered? You guessed it – Nate.

As we all waited on the side of the road, Nate drove back to look for Jay and the red van. About 20 minutes later he called me on the phone. He said the red van had just passed him and he was turning around to follow them back. But when the van got to our location, it kept going. It didn't stop. It was the wrong red van! Jay was still out there somewhere. So, Nate turned around and drove back again looking for Jay and the red van.

As we waited by the side of the road, Danny decided to teach all of us how to line dance. I still remember the puzzled looks we got from on-lookers as they drove by that morning and saw us line dancing on the side of the road in their small town in the middle of the Arizona desert.

After about 40 minutes, Nate called to say he couldn't find Jay anywhere. Then, as I was literally on the phone with Nate,

Jay suddenly appeared from the other direction in his red van. I didn't know what to think.

I asked Jay, "Where did you come from?"

He said, "I cut across the desert to surprise you at the gas station near the border. I thought it would be a good joke."

"What?" I exclaimed. "Why did you do that? This is a caravan."

"But it was a joke. I thought it would be funny," he said.

"What part of caravan don't you understand?" I asked. "By the way, where's your wife?"

Jay said, "I left her at the gas station by the border. She is really upset that I left the caravan. She stayed there in case you showed up at the gas station while I was out looking for you."

Since it was going to take Nate a while to drive back, I asked Jay if he and Danny would wait there for Nate while I took the other vehicles to the gas station to join his wife. As they waited for Nate to arrive, Jay said something to Danny that would mean much more to us later.

Jay told Danny, "I know I shouldn't have left the caravan. You wait and see. **God must have a reason for this.**"

I would learn over the years that Jay is a man who is completely devoted to God. He is a man of faith. God has worked powerfully through Jay and Rose for a long time.

Because of all the delays, we finally arrived at the border a little before 2:00 p.m. All of a sudden, there was another problem. The guards told us we couldn't come across the border with our lumber. They said we had to go home. Jay and Rose both speak Spanish fluently, so they asked the guards for permission to cross the border so we could build a house for the needy family. But the guards still said they wouldn't let us come into Mexico with the lumber. Jay and Rose continued to beg for permission to cross the border, but to no avail. The Mexican border guards would not be swayed. They insisted we could not cross the border.

After a while I remember thinking, "This has been interesting, but I think it's about time we get across."

All of a sudden, the director of the border appeared and told the guards, "It's okay. Pablo just called. These are friends of his. Let them cross."

Pablo had been Jay and Rose's friend for years. He lived in Mexico about 60 miles from the border. While Jay had been talking to the guards, Rose called Pablo to ask if he could help us get across the border. After making a few calls, Pablo called Rose back to tell her that a friend of his who worked at the border would be coming on duty soon for the 2:00 p.m. shift change. When the new crew arrived, Pablo called his friend to tell him who we were and we got permission to cross. We arrived at the border a little before 2 o'clock - 4 hours later than expected because of all of the delays that day. Without these delays, there is a very good chance that we might not have made it across the border with the lumber to build the first house. **Jay was right – God had a reason for delaying our trip to the border.**

If you are following God and encountering some difficulties, don't be surprised. Jesus said in the Bible *(John 16:33) that He wants us to have His peace. Then He said that while on this earth we will have many trials and sorrows. But we are to take heart because He has overcome the world.*

✤✤✤✤✤✤✤✤✤✤✤✤✤✤✤✤✤

If things aren't going according to your plans – trust God . . . trust His plan!

Chapter 6

The Rain

And we are confident that He hears us whenever we ask for anything that pleases Him. And since we know He hears us when we make our requests, we also know that He will give us what we ask for.
1 John 5:14-15

During all the years of doing ministry in Mexico, one memory stands out above all the rest. On one particular weekend trip, we wanted to bless a family by making repairs to their existing house. When we arrived, we asked a friend there if she knew of anyone whose home needed repairs. She said she did, then led us to a very poor part of town and introduced us to a woman who lived in a small house with her husband and young child. The young woman said that their roof leaked badly and was very happy when we told her that we would fix it.

Staying dry and warm during a rainstorm is something we, in the States, take for granted. Other people around the world aren't so fortunate. I've often thought about how hard it must be for a family to be inside their home with a roof that leaks and they cannot stay dry during a rainstorm.

After inspecting the roof, we realized that it would be better to replace the entire roof rather than try to repair it. The problem was that the old one had very little support and was made of small pieces of plywood and paper. It was so unstable that it wasn't safe for all of us to walk on. So, we decided to work on half of the roof at a time, using some of our lumber as columns to support that part of the roof, while a few of us walked on it. The rest of our group would work from ladders leaned against the side of the house. After we had removed and replaced the first half of the roof, we'd move the support columns to the other half of the roof and replace it the same way.

Things went according to plan as we began to remove the first half of the roof. But after we had completely removed that portion, we noticed a large rainstorm coming our way. The sky had suddenly turned very dark, the wind was strong and there appeared to literally be a wall of rain coming toward us. It was only a few blocks away and approaching rapidly!

My first thought was, "Oh no! We came here to help this family. Now everything they have inside their house will be soaked."

Then I thought, "Let's ask God to stop the rain."

"No," I thought, "we can't do that. If He doesn't stop the rain, I'll look pretty stupid. Besides, the people here need the rain. It's not their fault that we just removed half of this roof."

But I had a very definite feeling that God wanted me to ask Him to stop the rain.

I was on the roof at the time, so I called down to the group below, "Hurry! Pray! Ask God to stop the rain!"

The group on the ground below us formed a circle and began to pray as the two of us on the roof continued to work. When I glanced down a minute or so later, I saw that the group was continuing to pray. Then I did something I don't ever remember doing before. I felt as if God was telling me at that moment that He had heard us the first time and that we didn't have to ask Him again.

So, I interrupted the group and said, "God heard you the first time. Stop praying and get back to work."

I wouldn't usually interrupt someone while they were praying; but for some reason on that day in Mexico, it seemed as if God was prompting me to tell them to stop praying. So I did; then we all went back to work. After a while, we finished replacing the part of the roof we had removed. It was only then that I realized that we had been working for 20 to 30 minutes without being rained upon.

I looked up and was shocked by what I saw. Everywhere I looked we were surrounded by the storm and heavy rain. But there were only blue skies directly over us; the storm was all around us except where we were working! Although the entire neighborhood got soaked, our small area of a block or two never felt a drop!

So, what did we do? We removed the other half of the roof and replaced it also. As we were working, the woman's husband returned home from work. He was surprised and very grateful that we were repairing his roof. In fact, he jumped right in and helped us as we were finishing the job, while his wife and child looked on. We worked for a while longer, completely surrounded by the storm and never got wet. Then, the storm began to move away. It was then that I stopped working long enough to fully realize that the entire area around had been drenched for about an hour, but not us!

What we had just experienced was a dramatic, instant answer to prayer! I am often amazed by my God, but rarely as amazed as I was on that day.

The thought occurred to me, "We have seen such a remarkable thing today. I just bet that God did this for me to build my faith. He must know that a day is coming in the future when I will need additional faith." I'm sure the faith of the others was also strengthened that day.

Over the years, I've thought about that weekend in Mexico and how God answered our prayers as the storm was almost upon us. As I said earlier, I wouldn't usually interrupt anyone who is praying. There is certainly nothing wrong with praying continually for the same thing. Jesus taught about the benefits of taking our requests to God often. He taught us a lot about prayer.

I don't know all there is to know about prayer, but I've studied what the Bible says about it. And I know my God. I know He hears our prayers and He sees our hearts and our motives as we pray. I've seen Him answer many prayers over the years. I know I can trust Him and I can trust how and when He answers specific prayers. God wants us to share our thoughts with Him and ask for specific things as we pray. More than that, He wants us to spend time with Him in prayer – not as a ritual or obligation, but as two people who are in love and wanting to spend time together. As we do, He will hear the desires of our hearts. More importantly, we will learn to listen to the desires of His heart. Prayer is not a cosmic vending machine, where we get stuff we don't really need. **Prayer is talking with our Creator and allowing Him to change the desires of our heart to be more like His.**

I will always remember the day we went to Mexico as ambassadors for our God to bless a family, and God stopped the rain over our little area as we worked!

❧❧❧❧❧❧❧❧❧❧❧❧❧❧❧❧❧❧❧

As we are serving the Lord and seeking to glorify Him – let's be bold as we ask in faith for Him to act!

Chapter 7

Gregorio's Roof

And this same God who takes care of me will supply all your
needs from His glorious riches,
which have been given to us in Christ Jesus.
Philippians 4:19

As mentioned in a prior chapter, God used us to build 22 houses and repair 10 additional houses during about 4 ½ years of ministry in Mexico. Except for the small fund-raising event we did for the first house, we made no efforts to do any organized fund-raising events or make any special appeals for money to do these projects. God continually provided the people and the resources we needed.

One day, two people at my church each handed me an envelope saying, "Here. This is to help your efforts in Mexico."

As usual, I hadn't made any requests for money. I didn't even know these two people very well. I was surprised when I opened the envelopes – there were two checks inside totaling $ 4,000. I was accustomed to people sometimes giving me donations for Mexico but not donations of this size. It probably should've occurred to me that God was sending this money for a specific purpose, but it didn't.

During our next mission trip, I went to visit my dear friends, Gregorio and Maria Lupita. They really love God a lot. As a result of their love for Him, they have dedicated years of their lives to serving Him by helping people who were homeless and those fighting addictions. Years ago, when they first felt God calling them to ministry, they had no money and no training or education in this area of ministry. What they had was a deep faith in God and a desire to obey him.

When Gregorio built his first ministry building, he had no materials or help. He collected leftover scraps from construction sites and built a one-room structure, tying wooden pallets together and covering them with stucco to make the walls. The roof was built with a few pieces of lumber nailed together and covered with palmetto branches. **He used a rock to drive the nails because he didn't have a hammer; the same rock he used to straighten the old, bent nails he had found.**

When I stopped by to see Gregorio and his wife, he told me he had just been warned by the city officials that he had to replace the roof on his facility or they would shut him down. His people would be homeless again. I took a closer look at his roof and understood why the officials were concerned. The entire roof was unstable. It also was a fire hazard. A single electrical wire (with very little insulation) ran through the dry palmetto branches, connecting to a single bulb.

I told him we would return soon to remove the old roof, stabilize the walls and build a new roof. It was quite a big job for our team. As expected, God provided a large group of talented construction workers for that trip. When the weekend was over and the roof was completed, I added up all the receipts for the construction materials. Guess what the total cost was? Just a little less than $4,000.

Now I understood why two people were led to give me $4,000 at the exact time that Gregorio and Maria Lupita needed a new roof. I'm so glad they listened to God and obeyed. I'm so glad that Gregorio and Maria Lupita continue to obey God as He asks them to be His light to a dark place.

It has now been a few years since that roof was built. Since then, Gregorio and Maria Lupita's ministry has grown and they have built four more buildings to minister to people in their community.

I have very fond memories of stopping by to see them over

the years. Sometimes we met to do ministry together. Sometimes we just sat and talked, as friends do (fortunately Gregorio speaks English as well as Spanish). More than once, after talking for a while, we would open our Bibles to talk about what we had been reading that day. That would then lead us down a path of other verses, as we rejoiced in the promises that are found in the Bible. Our mutual love for our Lord and for the Bible is a big part of the special bond that we have. Like many of God's people, Gregorio and Maria Lupita go unnoticed by most of the world as they serve God faithfully. But they don't go unnoticed by God.

✿✿✿✿✿✿✿✿✿✿✿✿✿✿✿✿✿✿

Seek after the things of this world and you will miss God's best for your life.

Seek after God, His Kingdom and His right way of living, and He will give you what you need. (Matthew 6:33)

Chapter 8

Sometimes I Get in the Way

Each time He (God) said, "My grace is all you need.
My power works best in weakness."
So now I am glad to boast about my weaknesses,
so that the power of Christ can work through me.
2 Corinthians 12:9

There have been times when I've become aware of my imperfections while serving the Lord, often working with a lot of enthusiasm, but sometimes lacking the patience and love for others that Jesus demonstrated. I look back now and see times when my efforts to love people for Jesus would have been more effective if I'd been more focused on His plan, not my own. **There were times when I got in His way.**

This was especially evident one weekend in Mexico. For years, it had been our custom to help a local church there with a Saturday night service for the community. Usually, their pastor would preach; but this particular service would be different. We believed that God wanted us to bring in a guest speaker from the States. So, we began planning the event, even though we didn't know who the guest speaker would be.

We prayed for weeks, asking God to send us the man He wanted for the service. As usual, God exceeded our expectations. Someone told me about the pastor of a Hispanic church in Phoenix. His name was Raul and he had spent years preaching in Central and South America before coming to the U.S. From the first time I met Pastor Raul, I was immediately drawn to this man who was so full of joy and totally committed to serving our Lord. I was delighted when he said he would be the speaker at our upcoming event.

As we made plans, I felt the best way to advertise the service was to hire a truck to drive through the neighborhoods near the church. This was a common way of advertising in that town. We often saw them driving slowly up and down the streets of this town playing various announcements over loud speakers attached to the outside of their trucks.

Finally, the weekend for the special event arrived. On Saturday morning, I asked Pastor Carlos to make arrangements for the truck drivers to announce that the 6:00 p.m. service would have a special guest speaker from the States. Then, I went to help with the food distribution. This was one of my favorite things to do while in Mexico. Every month we worked together with people from the community, often packing and loading more than a hundred bags of groceries into our trucks to deliver throughout the area.

Then came the fun part. Before we left, neighborhood kids would playfully jump onto the back of our trucks and help as we went door-to-door. What a sight! Each truck filled with a mountain of "bolsas" (Spanish for bags), along with a "flock" of happy niños (boys and girls) – bouncing down a bumpy dirt road, kicking up a cloud of dust as we headed out to deliver the plastic bags that had been lovingly filled with potatoes, beans, flour and rice. But they were more than just bags of food. **They were a tangible reminder to the people of this community that they were loved by God.**

After we finished loading the food into our trucks, Dr. Bradford jumped into my truck. He heard that we were in town giving out food and wanted to join us. I had heard his name before, but I had never met him. He was a doctor from the States who had been making trips to Mexico for years to provide free medical care for the people there. I was really glad to meet him for the first time and have him ride with me.

Usually, the packing and distribution of food lasted about

4 hours. I expected to be done well before the evening service started, but this Saturday was different. As we drove to the first house, it began to lightly rain. But that was okay; none of us cared that we were getting wet as we went door-to-door to hand out food. **There are few things as satisfying as giving food to people who have very little to eat.**

As the day continued, I became increasingly concerned about how long it was taking to hand out all the food in my truck. I usually said very little as I moved from house to house, because I didn't speak much Spanish. Usually, I would hand someone a bag of food with a smile and say, "Como estas? Esto es un regalo de Dios. Dios te bendiga." That is Spanish for "How are you doing? This (bag of food) is a gift from God. God bless you." Then I would move on to the next house.

But on this day, Dr. Bradford would often spend 5 minutes or more with some of the families. You could see how much he loved the people as we went from house to house. He spoke Spanish fluently and after he handed someone a bag of food, he would talk to them for a while and offer to pray with them. I enjoyed watching how the people responded to him as he joyfully ministered to them in his gentle, humble manner. But I was also aware that we were running painfully behind schedule.

On this day, my focus was on completing the task; his focus was on the people. I was thinking mostly about their physical needs; he was thinking about **ALL** of their needs. Dr. Bradford was handing out food just like I was, but he was doing it with more love and compassion.

As we went from house to house, I looked at my watch often and realized that we would have trouble making it back to the church on time. But Dr. Bradford still continued to take his time as he stood and talked to the people and prayed with them. My thoughts were on completing this task and then moving on to the next event. I felt I needed to be at the church before the service began.

Finally, we made it back to the church a little after six o'clock. I was shocked! **There was almost no one there for the service!** When I found Pastor Raul, I discovered that he had spent the day with the Pastor Carlos. They had become good friends. Even now as they stood around smiling and talking, they didn't seem to be concerned at all that so few people were there for the service.

Then, I was told that they had decided not to hire the truck drivers to drive around the community making announcements about the service. I couldn't believe it! This was how I had planned to make sure the people in the area knew about the service. Instead, they went to a local radio station to make the announcement. While they were there, they were both interviewed about the evening event.

They had not followed my plan, and now it appeared that almost no one was coming to the service. I was angry! My frustration had been building for hours, as the food delivery dragged on. Nothing had gone according to my plan. I was upset. No, actually I was livid.

I knew I had to calm down, so I walked away. Then something happened that I didn't expect. **As I was walking, a wave of peace and calm came over me**. It was so overwhelming, it could only have come from God. In that moment, I realized how wrong I had been. Immediately, my anger was completely gone – replaced with remorse.

I wanted to get away with God for a while, so I hurried to my truck. I cried as I expressed my regret to Him for my attitude throughout the day. The events of the day were not about my plans being accomplished. They were about God's plans. This was all about God using us, as His ambassadors, to bring His light and His love to the people of this town.

"God, I'm sorry." I prayed, "Please forgive me. I've been so wrong. This day belongs to you, not to me. The service tonight belongs to you. If only one person shows up and they discover for the first time who you are, it will all be worth it. Please forgive me."

Guess what happened next? By 7:00 p.m., so many people showed up that every seat in the church was filled and people were standing in the aisles! Then, Pastor Raul spoke and more than 80 people decided to give their lives to Jesus and trust Him as their Savior. We had never seen that kind of response to the Gospel message before!

I still smile when I think about one of the things that happened during the service. There were so many people there that I didn't want to take one of the seats for myself. So I was sitting on the floor and leaning against the wall as Pastor Raul spoke. I guess I was a bit tired because I fell asleep during the service. All of a sudden, I was awakened abruptly by a little Mexican boy who plopped down onto my lap. I didn't know who he was, but he appeared to be about 2 years old and he was adorable with his little jeans and boots and his big cowboy hat. He sat there for a moment, and then he got up and ran away.

I will always remember what God did in the hearts of so many people that weekend. I will also remember what He did in my heart that weekend. I had forgotten that we are here to be used by God as He works His plan. We are not here to make our plans and then ask Him to bless them. It's not enough to just do good things for God. It's important that we do them with love – with His love and compassion. **You see, our plans sometimes fail . . . but God's love never fails.**

I am very aware of my faults. I remember the times when I got in the way of what God wanted to do. In spite of this, He patiently continues to teach me His ways while working through me. I know I am still a work in progress. How patient and loving He is as He continues His work in me!

BY THE WAY - I discovered later that there was a big parade that day on the other side of town. A lot of the people who lived around the church were not home that day because they went to see the parade. The ones who weren't at the parade were inside their homes because of the rain. If we had hired the trucks, very few people would have been outside their homes to hear the announcements. But people all over town heard the radio broadcast and many of them came to our service that night. Looks like God's plan for that day was better than mine. What a surprise, huh?

❦❦❦❦❦❦❦❦❦❦❦❦❦❦❦❦❦

May I suggest this prayer for all of us … if we really mean it … God, lead me and I'll follow. Help me love as You do. I belong to You … use me … I'm Your burro.

Chapter 9

Eddie

And the King will say, "I tell you the truth,
when you did it to one of the least of these
My brothers and sisters, you were doing it to Me!"
Matthew 25:40

One weekend, I went to Mexico with my daughter Jennifer and good friends Josh and Diana. This was not one of our regular mission trips. We wanted to "hang out with God" (Bible and prayer time), visit with some friends and have time on the beach. While we were there, we did one of our favorite things – we bought big bags of beans and potatoes and drove out to an extremely poor part of town and gave the food away. It was a great weekend!

As we packed to return home, we asked God to lead us to one more person who needed food. Then, we drove to the store to buy food for the person God would bring to us. While we were standing in the checkout line, I noticed a man in front of us who was extremely skinny. I saw that he was only buying a few items, but I didn't really pay a lot of attention to him. As we were leaving the store, I saw him again. He was walking very slowly, carrying his small bag of groceries.

Then I realized, "That's him! That's the guy we asked God to lead us to; the food we bought is for him!"

I knew I should race after him, but I froze. I felt sure God wanted me to go after him.

But I hesitated. I thought of all the reasons not to run after him:

"How do I explain to him why I'm running after him?"

"I don't speak Spanish well." "He'll think that I'm strange."

I knew God wanted me to go after him, but I hesitated. **Then, I saw my daughter racing toward him.** I hadn't said a word to her about going after him, but there she was, running down the street to catch up with him. Obviously, she felt the same way I did about God wanting us to help him. As I watched her run toward him, I thought, "Atta girl. I didn't obey God. You did!"

When Josh, Diana and I caught up with them, we gave him the food and offered to give him a ride home. His name was Eddie. After he hopped into my truck, something happened that seems a bit comical now. I knew we only had a few minutes to talk to him before we got to his home, and I wanted to offer him spiritual food as well as physical food. I wanted to know if he knew Jesus personally.

So after we talked with him for a few minutes (with our limited Spanish), I asked him, "Conoces a Jesus?" (Do you know Jesus?)

He thought for a moment then he said, "No, no conozco a Jesus. A donde vive?" (No, I don't know Jesus. Where does he live?) We were confused by his response.

Then, my daughter Jennifer said, "No, No . . . Conoces a Jesuchristo?" (Do you know Jesus Christ?)

With a smile on his face he said, "Si, Conozco a Jesuchristo." (Yes, I do know Jesus Christ.)

Jennifer realized that the name Jesus is a common name in Mexico. Eddie didn't understand at first that I was talking about Jesus Christ, the son of God. Again, I had demonstrated through my limited ability to speak Spanish and my limited knowledge of the Mexican culture that you don't have to be real smart to be used by God. He can use any of us … if we are willing to go where He sends us and love as He does.

I began to stop by to see Eddie every time I was in Mexico

(once or twice monthly). He was alone and very poor. I wanted to make sure he had enough food and clean drinking water. Eddie lived in a small camper trailer that a friend loaned to him, because he had no home of his own. Over time, he and I became good friends, in spite of the language barrier – he spoke no English and I spoke very little Spanish. As I write now, several things stand out in my memories of Eddie. **He always had such a big smile on his face every time I saw him. And he was so skinny.** He rarely wore a shirt and even though I saw him on a regular basis, I was often shocked by how skinny he was.

As time passed, it became obvious that he was not in good health. In fact, during the next year, he became very sick. Fortunately, one of my friends in Mexico (Blanca), checked on him regularly when we weren't there. Blanca is one of those special people who is used by God to help a lot of people. Two of my very good friends from Phoenix (Harold and Kathy) also checked on Eddie often when they were in Mexico. We were all very concerned about him as his health continued to deteriorate.

Then came the day I'll always remember. It was just a routine trip, leading the group down to Mexico. But as I pulled up to the community center on Saturday morning, Blanca hurried out to see me. I was barely out of my truck when she told me that Eddie had died a few days before.

I was instantly saddened by the news. My friend was gone. For more than a year, I had looked forward to visiting with him every time I was in Mexico. Whenever someone depends upon you for many of their needs, they become a meaningful part of your life. He was my friend – a friend I would miss.

Years later, Harold and Kathy told me that they had been with Eddie just before he died. He told them that he was ready to die and go be with Jesus.

Many people might see Eddie as just another poor person in a poor country. But God saw him as His child, in need of more than just food. Eddie needed friends, so God sent us. Isn't it great that Eddie wasn't alone at the end of his life?

God cares so much for all of us – especially the poor and needy. God wants and expects us to use our resources to help the poor *(1 Timothy 6:17-18 and Isaiah 58:7).*

ψψψψψψψψψψψψψψψψ

A thought occurred to me recently:

Like many Christians, I enjoy raising my hands when worshipping and praising God.

But there are times when God wants us to lower our hands and wrap our arms around someone in need.

That is truly an act of worship that pleases our Lord.

Chapter 10

Fire

The Lord is close to the brokenhearted;
He rescues those whose spirits are crushed.
Psalm 34:18

One day, during one of our trips to Mexico, we heard a loud noise outside the house where we were staying. We looked outside and saw that the electric transformer had exploded and caught on fire. The fire quickly went out by itself. But our house had lost its electricity, so we were forced to move to another house that was about one mile further west. We would later find out that God had a reason for us to be in the other house.

On Sunday morning, Rose spotted a young woman walking by the front of our house and said, **"I think that woman is crying."**

I looked outside, but I couldn't see if she was crying or not. Rose seemed certain that the woman was upset and crying, so I went outside to ask if she was OK. As it turned out, she had been crying. She said that her name was Mary and that she needed a ride back to her home in Arizona and wasn't sure how she would find one. I told her that I was with a church group from Arizona and we were leaving later that day to go back home. She seemed relieved to accept our offer when we invited her to ride back to Arizona with us.

Mary came inside and told us she had come to Mexico with her husband and a few friends to go to a rock and roll concert. In the middle of the night, she woke up to find that her husband wasn't asleep next to her. When she went to look for him, she found him on the beach kissing her best friend. She found out later that night that the two of them had been having an affair.

She was devastated. She had been walking up and down the road that morning, not knowing what she was going to do. Her husband and her friends told her she should forget about what had happened and just get over it. Her husband expressed very little regret about what he had done.

Even though she had no way to get home, she knew she was not going to ride back in the same vehicle with them. We took her back to where she had been staying so she could get her belongings and then we left for Arizona. It was a long drive home, so we had plenty of time to talk.

We discovered that she had been married for less than a year. As we talked about a number of things, we could see that she was really hurt by what her husband had done. So, we told her about how much our God likes to help all of us during our hardest times. She told us that she had decided to follow Jesus as a child, but she had turned her back on Him years ago. **Now, as we continued to talk, she thought it was time for her to turn back to God.**

After a while, we arrived in Phoenix and everyone went to their individual homes, except for me and my daughter. We drove our new friend to her home, which was in another city (about two hours from our town). It was late when my daughter and I finally got back home. We were tired, but so grateful that God had brought this young woman into our lives at a time when she really needed new friends and also needed to rediscover God's love for her.

We hoped her husband would realize how wrong he had been and would reconcile with her. But she called us later and told us they were splitting up. Mary had asked him to turn to God and begin marriage counseling with her. Unfortunately, he decided instead to divorce her and marry her best friend.

For quite a while, Mary stayed in touch with us although she lived in a different part of the state. She did return to a closer walk with God and started going back to church. Eventually, she moved to another state. I haven't talked to her in a while, but I'm so glad God used us to reach out to her and point her back to Jesus during one of the worst times of her life.

I will always be glad that the transformer caught on fire that day. Because of it, we moved to a new house located on the street where our new friend was walking that morning. I love to see how God rescues people who are in trouble.

🐴🐴🐴🐴🐴🐴🐴🐴🐴🐴🐴🐴🐴

God often wants to use us to rescue people in need.

What's your agenda today? Tomorrow?

Yours or His?

Chapter 11

Stranded

*. . . If we don't love people we can see,
how can we love God, whom we cannot see?*
1 John 4:20

There is an incident that happened while we were doing ministry in Mexico that I've thought about more than once over the years. As we did once a month, our group left Arizona after work on Friday, looking forward to another weekend of serving God in Mexico. We arrived a little after midnight at the place where we were staying for the weekend.

The next morning, we drove to the local church to start packing the bags of food we would take later that day to needy people in the community. As soon as we got there, someone told us that the pastor's brother needed to see us right away. When we went to see him, he introduced us to two American women and a small child who had become stranded there.

Apparently, one of the women got into a fight with her boyfriend while they were there on vacation. He got mad and drove home, leaving the three of them in Mexico. Their cell phones didn't have international service, so they couldn't call home. They also had very little money, so they couldn't buy bus tickets to get home. **They were stuck in Mexico with no way to return to Arizona.** More than that, they had no way to call their families to let them know they were safe or to call their bosses to explain why they weren't at work.

For days, they walked around town asking for help. All they wanted was a small loan so they could buy three bus tickets to get home. They promised to mail the money back to repay the loan as soon as they got home. **It seemed remarkable to me that no one offered to help – no one!** They went to some of the businesses in town and were turned away. They also went from church to church and still received no help.

However, someone at one of the churches had a suggestion: "No, we can't help you. But we know a church across town that likes to help people. Why don't you go there?"

It happened to be the church that had been built by Jay and Rose's ministry. So they went there and received help immediately. The pastor's brother and his family took them into their small house, giving them a place to stay and food to eat until we arrived the following weekend. Naturally, we took them to the bus station and bought the tickets they needed to get home.

The comment by the people at that church has stayed with me for years . . . "We can't help you. But we know a church that likes to help people."

If we think of the church as God's people throughout the world and not just a building, I wonder how often God's church (His people) have said the same thing or thought the same thing when seeing someone in need. I wonder how often I have said or thought the same thing . . . "I can't (or won't) help. Someone else can do that."

Next time we see someone in need:

Let's not be concerned about the cost (time and/or money)…

Let's not think about whether they deserve it or not…

Let's see them as Jesus being the one needing help – the same Jesus who willfully gave everything He had for you and me . . . when we didn't deserve it.

Jesus tells us in the Bible *(Matthew 25:34-46)* that when we do anything to help someone else, we are doing it to Him. If we refuse to help someone else in need, we are refusing to help Him. **One of the greatest callings any of us have in life is "to just show up" for those in need.** The same way Jesus did when He showed up in Bethlehem, and later at Calvary – because we needed Him . . .

We need to slow down and take our eyes off of ourselves. We need to notice the people around us and help them during their time of need . . . Jesus tells us to love our neighbors as we love ourselves.

❦❦❦❦❦❦❦❦❦❦❦❦❦❦❦❦❦

The next time you see someone in need . . .
The ball is in your court . . .
What are you going to do?

Chapter 12

The Meeting

*For Christ's love compels us, because we are convinced that
one died for all, and therefore all died. And He died for all,
that those who live should no longer live for themselves
but for Him who died for them and was raised again.
2 Corinthians 5:14-15 (NIV)*

One day I got a call from Megan. She was a teenager who had become a regular on our monthly trips to Mexico. One of the things that stood out about Megan was her love for the children we ministered to there and their love for her. For instance, there was the day in Mexico when we were all preparing to leave for the return trip home. As usual, Megan had a swarm of kids around her. They were OK with all of us leaving, but they didn't want her to leave. About a dozen kids jokingly formed a circle around her and interlocked their arms, trying to prevent her from leaving. Finally, after some effort on our part and protests on their part, they finally released her and let her get into one of our cars so that we could leave for home. We all enjoyed seeing how much they loved Megan.

Back to the call . . . Megan asked if I could meet with her as soon as possible. She said she had something very important to ask me. It sounded like there was a major issue in her life, so we scheduled a time to meet right away.

When we met, our initial conversation started out very casually. I was really concerned about her and wanted to know what was so urgent. So, after a few minutes, I asked her if there was something specific she wanted to discuss. Her response surprised me. She told me that she thought she wasn't doing enough for God and asked me if I knew of any ministry opportunities for her.

As we talked, it was obvious to me that she wanted to do more for her Lord because of her love for Him – not out of a feeling of obligation or a need to perform. Hearing her talk so passionately about wanting to do more to serve God put a big smile on my face – I'm sure it did the same for Him too. As we talked, I was relieved that there was no major crisis in her life. But more than that, I was touched by her love for Jesus and her desire to serve Him. She was compelled by her love for Jesus to live for Him and not for herself *(2 Corinthians 5:14-15)*. In her own way, she was saying that she was a burro for Jesus just like I was – she belonged to Him for His use.

Although I knew of several ministries she could join, I suggested we pray about this and wait to see what the Lord had planned for her. As a result of subsequent prayers and meetings – a new ministry quickly emerged! Within a few months, we would send a team to Mexico for 10 days or so to conduct a week-long Vacation Bible School (VBS) for the kids and the parents there. VBS – a week full of games, singing, arts & crafts, puppet shows, food and more! Preparing for the event was a big effort. We would be serving food to more than 100 people daily as well as getting ready for the other activities.

What a week it was – full of laughter and fun, teaching about the love of God, and developing relationships as we worked side by side with the people from the local church there. Megan was a key part of this ministry for many years.

I have so many wonderful memories of VBS in Mexico: the many hours spent making what seemed like thousands of PB&J sandwiches, the day Kristen went on a rampage and swatted more than 100 flies in our house (she actually counted them), the laughter of the children, line dancing with the adults and children up and down the church aisles and the puppet shows, just to name a few.

One of the highlights of VBS every year was the puppet shows. We used the puppets to teach Bible lessons each day, to the delight of the children and adults who attended. The puppet shows were truly a result of teamwork. Josh originally suggested the idea. In fact, he eventually got the nickname "muppet man" (the people in Mexico called them "muppets" instead of puppets).

Then, Stephen came over to my house in Phoenix before our first VBS and showed me how to build a puppet stage that was easy to disassemble and transport, using PVC pipes and sheets.

When we needed someone from our group who spoke spanish to rehearse the skits with the "puppeteers" from the church in Mexico, Holly and Sam stepped forward. They did such a wonderful job working with all the volunteers as well as being the moderator of each show, as the people behind the curtains of the home-made stage used the puppets to entertain the audience with skits that taught biblical truths. Each puppet show was filled with laughter and music and was made possible by so many people from both sides of the border working together.

Then, there was the night when none of the volunteer workers wanted to leave the church after VBS. We stayed there for a long time (some of us from the U.S. and some from the local church) – talking and playing loud music and dancing.

Then, when Pastor Carlos wanted to pray, we joined hands in a circle and there was prayer unlike anything I've ever experienced before or since. I don't know if I can find the words to adequately describe what happened but I'll try. The men and women from Mexico didn't take turns praying one at a time as we often do here in the States. They began to all pray loudly at one time – an orchestra of voices joyfully expressing their love to their Heavenly Father. I could feel the sweet presence of the Holy Spirit as their voices melded together in unison and grew in intensity. **I could only imagine the joy our Lord felt as the**

sweet aroma of His people's prayers rose to Him in Heaven. It reminds me of *Revelation 8:4 – "The smoke of the incense, mixed with the prayers of God's holy people, ascended up to God from the altar where the angels had poured them out."*

The week long VBS was something we looked forward to each year. Eventually, Megan and I both stepped away from the Mexico ministry – to do ministry in the U.S. She also became involved with a ministry in Africa. Today, the ministry in Mexico continues without us and VBS stands out as one of the highlights every year. It began many years ago because of a young woman's desire to do more to please her Lord. It continues today to be a very meaningful part of touching lives for Jesus.

Although my role in all of this was very small, I include it in this book because it's such a good example of how God touches lives through any of His followers who are truly devoted to Him and offer themselves to Him for His use.

♙♙♙♙♙♙♙♙♙♙♙♙♙♙♙♙♙♙

Oh! That our passion would be for Jesus and we would continually look for new ways to please Him!

Oh! That we would all see the fullness of God's glory and turn our eyes off of ourselves and onto Him and others!

Chapter 13

The Accident

. . . mourn with those who mourn.
Romans 12:15 (NIV)

We heard about the accident. Two people on a motorcycle were hit by a drunk driver and killed as they sat at a traffic light in Phoenix, Arizona. We saw the family's grief and pain every time we passed that corner. For years they marked the accident site often with fresh flowers, new candles and pictures. Their pain was obvious. I prayed for them often although I didn't know who they were. I asked God to send someone to them – someone who would tell them about His love and His comfort in the midst of their grief. **I didn't know that I would be one of the ones He would send to them.**

A few years later, Rose and I were returning home from a mission trip in Mexico. After we crossed the border into Arizona, we passed a truck on the side of the road with the hood raised. As we raced past, I felt we should turn around and see if we could be of any help. I'm so glad we did! A man was stranded there, with his young grandson, in an area where his cell phone had no service. His truck needed a new belt to replace the one that was broken and the nearest auto parts store was about 30 miles away. So we all jumped into my truck and off we went.

As we drove along and talked, the young boy was sitting on Rose's lap because my truck only had one seat for the four of us. While Rose was talking to him, he told her that his dad was in Heaven. The grandfather explained that the boy's father (his son-in-law) had been killed in a motorcycle accident. As he described the accident, I realized that they were a part of the family I had prayed for all of these years!

Rose and I listened as he told us about the accident and about his family. He listened as we told him about our God and the comfort He provides to those who turn to Him for help. We talked about Jesus and how He came to give us an abundant life – a life full of hope and purpose for all who believe in Him. Our new friend was not sure what he believed about Jesus, but he listened as we talked to him about the new life we can all experience through faith in Jesus.

After a while, we made it back to his truck and replaced the broken belt. I wanted to talk with him more, but it was time for all of us to leave, so I asked him if we could meet sometime soon. He said we could and we did meet for lunch a few days later. I listened as he told me more of his story and he listened as I told him more about Jesus. It was a good conversation, but he made no decision that day about Jesus.

I haven't seen him for years. I don't know if he ever made a decision to follow Jesus and receive the new life that Jesus promises. I hope so. I pray so. As you read this, please pray the same for him and his family. Our God is good and He hears our prayers. I know He'll send someone else to help this family.

❧❧❧❧❧❧❧❧❧❧❧❧❧❧❧❧❧❧

Pray often . . . Prayer is an intimate time with our Heavenly Father.

I've got an idea...PRAY NOW...before you read on.

If you're not accustomed to praying, that's OK. Your prayer doesn't have to be elaborate. Just talk to God as if He's right there with you – because He is!

He's waiting to hear from you!

A BURRO FOR JESUS

Chapter 14

God's Special Delivery

*And my God will meet all your needs according to
the riches of His glory in Christ Jesus.
Philippians 4:19*

I was talking with a friend, as we were discussing our
plan to help someone who was facing a very difficult time. "This
is great," he said. "Have you ever done anything like this before?"

"Yes, I'm lucky," I replied. "I'm part of a ministry that
likes to help people. For years, we have asked God to send us
people who need help and then we ask Him to send us what
they need. And He does."

"I want to do more of this," he said.

I knew this was not his first time helping someone. But I
also knew what He meant. Every time God sends me to someone's aid, I love being a part of what He's doing in their life.
**I love being used by God as He reaches out to someone in
need.**

I've often wondered why I'm so lucky. Why does God
notice me? Why did he invite me to become part of His family?
Why did He choose me to be a part of His plan to rescue people
in trouble and to take His message of love to so many people? It
can only be explained by His grace and His love for me.

There have been many times when people have thanked
me after we have helped them. I would accept their thanks, then
often tell them what I knew to be true:

"The real thanks goes to God. He saw you in trouble. He
had what you needed and He asked us to deliver it to you. We are

only the delivery boys. God is the one we should be thanking."
**Delivery boys (and girls) . . . modern day words for "burro".
Delivery boys and girls for God . . . it's a great job!**

One very special delivery stands out in my memory. We had tried unsuccessfully for more than a year to get a shipment across the border into Mexico. Although we had written permission from Mexican officials to bring it into Mexico, the border guards wouldn't allow it. The shipment contained hundreds of boxes from World Missionary Press. Each box was filled with hundreds of Christian missionary booklets printed in Spanish. We estimated that these pallets of boxes had more than 400,000 individual booklets of various types.

One day Jim called me about the shipment that was still in the U.S. Jim is one of my dearest friends. He's another one of those people who the world does not notice, but God does – as they work tirelessly for God because of their love for Him. When Jim felt God calling him to become a full time missionary in Mexico – he went there, with no financial support and without knowing anyone there.

He's now been in Mexico more than 20 years. While living there as a missionary, he's been stabbed twice and shot once. **He's also seen one of his best friends killed because he left the drug cartel to become a Christian.** Jim is now in his 50's and living with cancer. He has very little income or personal belongings. He has no retirement plan and no health insurance. What he has is a genuine faith in God and the joy of Jesus in his life – something that is much better than anything money can buy. He works happily every day in a ministry that he and God started years ago – a ministry that has grown to now impact the entire country of Mexico, as he coordinates the delivery of World Missionary Press materials to thousands of pastors in Mexico. Jim remains single-minded in his obsession for God and his commitment to serve Him. Jim would be the first to say that all the glory goes to God for anything that has been accomplished through the years of ministry there. In Mexico, Jim is called Santiago, so I'll use that name also as I write this, because I'll be mentioning another friend later who is also named Jim.

Back to the call from Santiago. He said that he now had a way to get the boxes across the border. So, with the help of my friends Henry, Jim, Mark and Stephen, I rented a large truck and we set off to a small town near the border where we had stored the boxes for a long time.

After we had loaded about half the boxes, Jim (my USA friend) realized we would exceed the weight limit of the truck if we loaded all the boxes. We couldn't load the rest of the boxes and safely transport them to their destination. We also couldn't leave the remaining boxes where they were. The owner of the storage units wanted us to remove all the boxes since he would soon be selling the business to a new owner.

We couldn't overload the truck and we couldn't leave the extra boxes in storage. Then we had an idea. We decided to drive the partially loaded truck to a nearby town and expect God to help us find someone who wanted the ministry materials. When we arrived at a local church, one of the people there called a lady in their congregation who did ministry in Mexico. The woman drove over immediately, and was overjoyed when we told her what we had in the truck.

She told us that she and her husband had left higher paying jobs to move closer to the border because they wanted to do ministry in Mexico. It took a lot of their income to cover the travel expenses, food and other supplies they took into Mexico. They didn't have enough money left over for the many Bibles and Christian books they needed for ministry, but they had been praying to God about their needs. Now, here we were with more than a hundred boxes filled with scripture booklets as well as an assortment of ministry items printed in Spanish.

What a moment we had – celebrating the goodness of our God and how He provides. What a joyful moment for this woman who had prayed and now had received her answer – a special delivery from God for the people in Mexico . . . trucked right to her doorstep, free of charge. After unloading everything at her house, we drove away, in awe of our Lord and how He orchestrated this whole thing to provide for this married couple, as they humbly did the work of their Lord in Mexico.

Then, we loaded the remaining boxes into the truck and drove several hours to the designated spot at the border. We also called a friend later who said he would bring more Spanish bibles to this couple to help with their ministry in Mexico.

❦❦❦❦❦❦❦❦❦❦❦❦❦❦❦❦❦❦

By the way, if you are not aware of World Missionary Press and their amazing ministry of printing and shipping Christian booklets (in a variety of languages) to missionaries and pastors around the world – check it out at www.wmpress.org. If you are looking for a very productive ministry that you can support with your prayers and your money – one that has a big impact on the building of God's kingdom – consider World Missionary Press. I am not a part of their ministry but I have seen the results of their work. You will also as you read the next chapter.

❦❦❦❦❦❦❦❦❦❦❦❦❦❦❦❦❦❦

All followers of Jesus are all called to deliver God's gifts - His comfort, forgiveness, grace, healing and provision . . . to those we meet.

Let's do it !

Chapter 15

Emails From Mexico

So shall My word be that goes forth from
My mouth; It shall not return void,
but it shall accomplish what I please...
Isaiah 55:11 (NKJ)

I recently received two emails from some friends in Mexico that have an amazing story to tell. These two separate emails show the power of God's written word to change lives. In each of these cases, the scripture booklets that are mentioned were supplied by World Missionary Press. I've changed the names of the two pastors and the cities mentioned because some of the pastors and missionaries in Mexico have been threatened by members of the Mafia (their name for the drug cartel). In spite of the risks, many continue to joyfully distribute the word of God throughout the entire country, as they tell people about God's love. Although I've changed the names below, the rest of the emails are typed exactly as they were when I received them (spelling and punctuation is in its original state):

Email # 1 - from a pastor in Mexico to the ministry providing scripture booklets.

"We now have been receiving material, scripture booklets, and bible studies from you guys for two years, our people are out every afternoon going door to door handing out scripture booklets. And yes we have had some problems from time to time for instance one day I went to a house and said hello and could I have a glass of water the lady said yes one minute, when she returned she said sit down on a bench in the front of the house and we visited which is normal and in our conversation I asked if I could give her something she said yes, so I reached into my bag and handed her a scripture booklet, she looked at it and said I should wait a minute for her husband to come out. So I sat there in the shade of the tree, in a few minutes her husband came out holding a pistol and told me this is what I think of your God and shot me in the leg, they had to remove my leg from the knee down. Sounds bad? Well I still pastor my church and it has not slowed me down, about six months later as I was walking down the street using crutches, I saw the lady and she came up to me running I thought oh lord here goes another leg. But she said sir my family has been mafia for many years and my husband shot you but you left the scripture booklet How To Know God and as time pasted we read it and the words in that booklet changed our lives our whole family accepted Jesus in our hearts and if you would could you supply us with a supply of these booklets to hand out, I said gladly. You see friends to many the cost was great but for me the blessings were far greater I would gladly give my other leg or even my life to see the light of Christ move in someone's life. The man who shot me has a very strong group in his house and they hand out around 200-300 booklets a day. Thank you for being in Mexico and supplying Mexico with these life giving booklets. Pastor Jose.

Email # 2 –
from a ministry in Mexico that distributes scripture booklets
Like to share a little of pastor, his name is Pablo his church is in Guaymas. He is from Panama, came from Panama, with his wife and four kids, in hopes of he and family crossing in to the US, as so many come up the same with the golden dream of life in the US. But as for Pablo and so many focus on the world, dreams gone bad, you see on the way up his wife and four kids were killed at the hands of the narco traffic. He was thinking

considering taking his life, but on the streets he received a little scripture booklet produced by World Missionary Press, and the spirit of God through the written word went to work on him. He has been pastoring his little church now which he planted with no support, but lots of faith 10 years ago with 5 or 6 home groups as well. Two years ago Pablo contacted me begging for scripture booklets and I mean begging, for the life giving written word. They are out daily distributing scripture booklets, please consider praying for pastor Pablo and his work. And if you pray for us as we labor together in the name of the lord our fruits are yours as well.

Message from Bert Hunt
     I don't know these two pastors personally but I know Santiago (the missionary mentioned in the prior chapter) very well and he knows them through his ministry in Mexico. For years I have seen and heard about the fruit of Santigo's ministry as he helps pastors throughout Mexico and provides scripture booklets to them that he receives from World Missionary Press.

ψψψψψψψψψψψψψψψψ

Please pray for Santiago and the missionaries and pastors in Mexico and for World Missionary Press.

Chapter 16

New Assignment

By faith Abraham . . . obeyed and went, even though
he did not know where he was going.
Hebrews 11:8 (NIV)

During the years I was helping to lead groups to Mexico, I occasionally experienced a little opposition from people in the U.S.A. Two conversations stand out in my mind as I write this. In both cases, the men made it very clear that I should be helping the poor here in the United States, not helping "those people" in another country.

In each case, I listened patiently for a while and then I responded by saying, "First of all, we're the ones who draw boundaries to separate countries. I believe God sees everyone in the world the same way – as people created in His image. He loves us all."

"Secondly," I continued, "I go to Mexico because that's where I believe God has sent me. He's the one who decides where He sends us to serve Him and minister to others. So I'll continue to go there unless He reassigns me."

My answer didn't satisfy either man. One of them actually got very angry with me after I told him that maybe the reason he felt so strongly about someone going to help a specific group of poor people in Texas was because God wanted him to go there to help them.

I assumed God would always have me involved with ministry in Mexico. The ministry had grown and was being used by God to bless so many of us (on both sides of the border). Besides that, I loved it so much. Surely, He wanted me to serve

Him there for the rest of my life.

But God had other plans. After about five years of doing ministry in Mexico, I sensed that God was telling me that what I had been doing was good, but it would end one day. I assumed this meant that it would end many years in the future. But after a while, I felt that God wanted me to resign soon from the Mexico ministry. So, I began to pray about someone to take my place in the ministry.

I'll probably always remember the morning I was sitting in my truck outside my church in Phoenix. I wasn't thinking about Mexico at the time. In fact, I was praying about the class I'd be teaching later that morning. When all of a sudden the thoughts that came to me from God were very direct and very clear.

There was no doubt in my mind that God was telling me, **"You don't look for your replacement – I do. If I tell you to resign . . . then you resign."**

As soon as church was over, I called the founders of the Mexico ministry (Jay and Rose) and asked if I could stop by to see them later that day. When I got to their house and they invited me inside, I said, "Before I sit down, let me tell you why I'm here. I'm here to resign."

"We know," Rose said. "For several months we have been sensing from God that He would be moving you on to something else." We talked for a moment longer and I thanked them for how God had used them and their ministry to impact my life. Then I left.

So that settled it. I was being reassigned by God, but I didn't know what my new assignment would be. This would be a big change for me. I thought about my friends in Mexico who I wouldn't see as often. I also thought about my American friends here who had gone with me on so many trips. Although I would probably see them occasionally, this would be a big change for all of us. I knew I would miss the ministry and my friends. Hundreds of people on both sides of the border had given their time, their talent and money to make the ministry happen.

The thought of leaving the ministry felt strange to me. It was an emotional time. I felt the sadness that comes from leaving people who are dear friends. I also felt the void that happens when things in our lives change and we leave something that is very familiar for something that is new. Even so, I was surprised how easy it was to say yes to God and resign from something that had been such a big part of my life. **It was easy because I loved God more than I loved the ministry.** He was **AND IS** the love of my life. I was entering a new chapter of my life, but I was going there with Jesus, my best friend. The sadness of the change was replaced with the anticipation of what would follow.

We all have many memories from the trips to Mexico. There was the night we tried to sleep outside when a tropical storm was nearby. The wind and noise that night was amazing. There were the food fights we sometimes had as we were driving home (my favorite was when my daughter took chocolate cookies apart and stuck them all over the outside of my truck – giving my truck a lot of polka dots). There were the two dogs – the one that chased me out of the field I shouldn't have been in anyway and the dog that bit me (followed ten days later by a trip across the border – ordered by the doctor to make sure the dog wasn't rabid).

There was the time I was going to Mexico by myself for a day. While I was there, I gave away food to a number of families. On my way out of town, I stopped by a house that we had built a year or so before and gave about a dozen potatoes to the kids who were there. The following week I found out that their mother had lost her job and they had almost no food. That family of six tried to make those potatoes last all week until our group arrived the following weekend with more food.

There were many late nights, after working all day in the community, when no one in our group wanted to go to sleep because we wanted to sing Christian songs and share Bible verses together. There were countless hours with Pastor Carlos as I watched his obvious love for the people of his community and his tireless energy.

There was that very special night at Gregorio's place when our group joined him and his neighbors for an evening of food and an evening of singing songs to God and sharing Bible verses with each other. We spoke the verses and sang the songs in both Spanish and English, but that night we were not Americans and Mexicans. We were all children of God singing and speaking out of love for our Heavenly Father in different languages. The presence of the Holy Spirit was so sweet that night that we didn't want to stop.

There was the house built during the sand storm, the school house built for the disabled children, the house built for the family who lost their home to a fire, the large activity center built to serve the community (with Blanca serving as the director of the center), the house built for the transvestite man and the house built by some of our friends for the drug dealer's family.

Some people might think we shouldn't build houses for people with questionable lifestyles. **However, our job as Christians is to love the people God puts in our lives (while sharing God's truth with them) . . . not judge them.** We decided to build houses for the people God led us to, and then leave the results to Him. More than once we saw people (including the drug dealer) turn from their old life to seek a new life with God after He used us and others to show His love for them in tangible ways.

There were many times when we experienced the satisfaction of helping people who had very little. Let me share one of those moments with you. We had driven a truck that was piled high with clothes to a remote area of town. People crowded around, delighted that they could take whatever they wanted, as a gift from us. When everything was gone and we were driving back, we came upon a little old woman dragging a huge, black plastic bag (overstuffed with the clothes she got from us) down a dirt road. She stood about 5 feet tall and the bag appeared to be at least 3 feet high. It probably weighed about half of her weight. She couldn't carry it. In fact, she could barely drag it. But she was laboring to pull it inch by inch, obviously determined to get it home, no matter how long it took. So, we offered her a ride home and as we were driving and talking, we found out she had very little food at her house.

We decided to really bless her and let her get as much food as she wanted at a nearby store. While we were there we were treated to a remarkable sight. Please picture this in your mind as I try my best to describe what happened. The tiny woman was carrying the small basket provided to all shoppers, as the four of us walked down the aisle. Every time she saw something she wanted, she showed it to us and asked "OK?" (I think this may be the only English word she knew). By the fourth or fifth time she asked "OK" and we answered "Si" (yes), she realized we were going to buy anything she wanted. Then, to our surprise and to our delight, she set the basket down and this petite, elderly lady started to literally dance up and down the aisle.

It was priceless! The Bible is correct – it is more blessed to give than to receive *(Acts 20:35)*.

Back to my decision to resign from the Mexico ministry. I didn't know what God wanted me to do next, but that was OK. He knew what He had for me in the future. I didn't need to know what He had planned for me until He wanted to tell me. I felt a little bit like Abraham in the Bible when he left home with his family to go to another land promised to him by God. The Bible said that Abraham left, not knowing where he was going *(Hebrews 11:8)*.

I get a bit emotional when I think about the next two

years. For those two years I received no clear direction from God about a new ministry assignment. But it was such a sweet time of resting (both physically and spiritually) while I was waiting on and seeking God. It was a precious time with my Lord – reading the Bible, praying and enjoying my time with Him. It was a time of growing in His grace and in my knowledge of Him. *(2 Peter 3:18).*

It was clear to me that God wanted me to slow down and spend more time with Him. **We can sometimes be so focused on doing good things that we miss the best things in our lives.** God doesn't need our activity; He wants our hearts and our love. Then, as we abide with Him, He produces results through us – in His timing *(John 15:5).* **We are then active with Him not just active for Him.**

God had other reasons for me to be in the U.S. instead of being in Mexico so often. My business wasn't doing well, so my finances were not in good shape. My health was even worse. Within a few months I would be in the hospital for about the fifth time in five years. Only this time was different. The medicine was not working well during the first week I was in the hospital. I wasn't sure that I was going to make it out of the hospital alive this time. Although I felt like I was too young to die, it was really exciting to think that I might die soon and actually see Jesus, the love of my life. I didn't have a death wish or anything like that. But the thought of seeing Jesus in person was thrilling. He obviously didn't want me to join Him in Heaven yet, or I wouldn't be writing this book. But that was OK too, because now I could serve Him longer before going to see Him. About this same time, my grandson was diagnosed with autism. And then several of the members of my family developed a renewed hunger for God. I was able to be here in Arizona with my family during all these events – both the good and the bad.

I believe God wanted me back in the U.S. for all the reasons mentioned in the paragraph above. But mostly, He wanted me to spend time with Him. **How amazing that the Creator of this universe notices you and me out of the billions of people on the Earth.** His desire is for us to spend time with Him. Wow! Makes you love Him even more, doesn't it?

By the way, after this period of resting in Him, He did eventually lead me to other ministry. Some of these adventures (after my time in Mexico) are included in the next section of this book.

"God . . . Thank You for those five years in Mexico – for using them to change me and teach me that everything I am and everything I have is because of You – given to me by You. I now offer them back to You for Your use. I belong to You – not to myself. My time, my money, my heart – I give to You. You freed me from a life of being enslaved by my own self-centered wants and desires. You gave me a new life that is free . . . free to love like You do, free to give like You do . . . a life filled with Your love and joy. A life with no fear and no worry. You gave me life the day I was born. Then you gave me a new spiritual life the day I decided to follow Jesus and I was reborn into Your family."

"God . . . I don't know what is in my future. But I know You. And I know You will be there in the future with me. So there is nothing to be anxious about, nothing to fear . . . Thank you."

🌱🌱🌱🌱🌱🌱🌱🌱🌱🌱🌱🌱🌱🌱🌱

Dear reader – God has a plan for your life. Don't worry about the future. Trust Him! Follow Him!

A family's home in Mexico.
(chapters 4,5)

A family's home in Mexico. (chapters 4,5)

Building the first
house in Mexico.
(Chapters 4,5)

A BURRO FOR JESUS

Fixing roof surrounded
by a storm.
(Chapter 6)

Building new house near the family's old house. (shack) (Chapter 4, 5)

A new house next to family's old house. (shack) (Chapter 4,5)

 A BURRO FOR JESUS

"Bolsas"– Bags of food
ready for delivery
(Chapter 8)

Diana (white shirt) and Jennifer delivering food
bags in Mexico. (Chapters 8,9)

Eddie (chapter 9)

Kelly (artist of burro sketch on title page) handing out clothes in Mexico.
(Chapter 21, 24, 35)
A BURRO FOR JESUS

Gregorio's original roof. Gregorio
standing by Coke machine.
(Chapter 7)

Fixing Gregorio's roof. (Chapter 7)

Gregorio's new roof (Chapter 7)
Night of praise (Bert with Bible, Gregorio behind Bert)
(Chapter 16)

 A BURRO FOR JESUS

Julie and Jennifer
(Chapter 27, 32)

Mike
(Chapter 19)

Laura and John
(Chapter 17)

Being a Burro for Jesus
in the U.S.A.

Chapter 17

No Longer Alone

Jesus said . . . I am with you always . . .
Matthew 28:20

I recently asked Laura if she would help me tell her story in this book.

Laura

"My husband Ray was my best friend for 33 years. He was the best thing that ever crossed my path. No one had ever loved me as Ray did. He treated me like a princess, from the beginning to our last days together."

"After Ray's passing, I felt lost, overwhelmed with loneliness and the responsibilities that I would have to take on by myself. I'd have to work everything out on my own. I was wondering how I would pay the bills with just one Social Security check coming in. I knew I'd have to start looking for work soon. I was afraid to start life over, like when you were young and had to get out into that busy, fast moving world by yourself."

"One month after Ray's passing, I called a dear friend, John. I didn't call to ask him for money or help, just some comforting advice. He called me back a little after that first conversation and asked if he could bring a friend by to talk with me. That's when I met Bert."

Bert

John and I met to talk and pray before we drove to Laura's house. This was such a bad time in her life. We knew we were intruding during her time of grief, but we wanted her to know that we were available to help. So, we went to see Laura;

not to give her a lot of quick answers but to listen to whatever she wanted to share with us.

As she talked about her life with Ray, it was obvious that she felt alone and was overwhelmed with her present circumstances. She said that she had very few friends except Ray and now he was gone. Her most immediate financial need was to pay the house payment that was due soon. She was not accustomed to making financial decisions and paying bills or even balancing a check book. Ray had always done all of those things. Fortunately, her sister was flying to town to be by Laura's side during this difficult time. Laura knew she would eventually have to go back to work (at least part time), but it was obvious to us that she needed some time to deal with the shock and grief she was experiencing, before starting back to work. She was in her mid 60's and hadn't worked in years.

Laura didn't ask for anything when we met, but John and I knew that God had sent us there to help. I told her that I was a part of a ministry that likes to help people. As a group, we would like to help her with her mortgage payment until she was ready to look for a job.

I remember Laura asking, "You mean people I don't even know are going to help me?"

"Yes."

"Why would they do that?"

"Because God wants us to help each other. He wants you to know that you are not alone in this."

"Who are these people?"

"I don't know yet, but God does. He'll let John and I know who they are. He wouldn't have sent us to you if He didn't plan to help you."

As I spoke to her, I knew that we had almost no money in the ministry account at that time. But I wasn't concerned about that because I knew God would send people to help –

that's who He is and that's what He does. I knew He would help, not only with financial support, but more importantly, with Christian women who would become a new circle of friends for Laura . . . her new family.

Laura

"John and Bert collected donations from people all around for the garage sale, all strangers who cared and wanted to help. They also helped pay some of my bills for a while. I still don't know who a lot of these people are who helped me. I know that they were sent to help me through God and His helpers, John and Bert."

Bert

Very quickly, God came through with more than we expected. No surprise there . . . but WOW! He did so much . . . through so many – so quickly. People donated time and money and some even donated things to the garage sale that Laura had planned in an effort to raise money for the upcoming bills. More than that – their efforts helped Laura realize that God saw her during her time of need and that she was not alone.

At the end of our first meeting, Laura asked John and I where we went to church and if she could join us there the next morning (which happened to be Sunday). Although she knew John and I went to the same church, we had said very little about our church because we didn't want her to think that she had to come to our church to get help from us. She said that she had not been to church in years but she wanted to join us on Sunday. So she did, and within a short time she joined the women's Bible study. The ladies in the Bible study have been such a meaningful part of God's team to love and accept Laura from that very first Sunday. **How pleased our God must have been as He watched people from His church be such a tangible proof of His love for Laura.**

Laura

"From that day in August, a lot of my stress and worries started to go away. I'm working now. My walk with God before losing Ray was not as strong as it is now. I've now been attending church and the Bible study regularly. This has helped me so much – meeting new people who have been caring friends, which I've never had before – all of which has brought me closer to God. I truly believe God is here for me each and every day."

Closing words from Laura

"Each day is different, some days are not as good as others. But, I now have hope and faith for tomorrow. I now want to become stronger, so I will someday be able to walk with someone who's having trouble getting through each day, and let them know how there is hope and better days to come."

"I'm still lonely at times and have my moments. But, I then remember that God is always going to be by my side, so I'm not really alone . . ."

Bert

Thank You, God, for bringing us into Laura's life and for bringing her into our lives. She is such a blessing to all of us who know her.

✿✿✿✿✿✿✿✿✿✿✿✿✿✿✿✿

**We are here to love Jesus and to love others for Jesus –
So let's do it joyfully.**

Chapter 18

Bedbugs

The Lord . . . is patient with you, not wanting anyone
to perish, but everyone to come to repentance.
2 Peter 3:9 (NIV)

One day, as I was driving some friends home, they told me that their neighbor, Jimmy, was in the final stages of cancer and not expected to live much longer. They also told me that he was not a Christian.

After I dropped them off, I felt like God wanted me to talk to Jimmy. I was concerned that he might die soon and never find the peace of knowing God personally and living with Him in Heaven for all of eternity. I was a bit nervous as I walked to his apartment because it might seem a bit odd to him that a complete stranger would come over to visit with him. Even though I wasn't sure what I would say to him, I was sure God wanted me to talk to him. So I went over and knocked on his door.

When he opened the door, I said, "Hi. I'm sorry to interrupt you. I know you don't know me, but I heard from my friends that you have cancer. It may seem a little strange that I would come talk to you like this, but I like to pray. I was wondering if it would be okay with you if I prayed for you."

I was glad when he said I could pray for him and he invited me inside. We talked for a few minutes then I prayed for him. As we continued to talk, he told me about his life and his family. Before I left, I said that one of my favorite things to do was to read the Bible. I asked him if it would be okay if I came over regularly after work so that he and I could read the Bible together. I told him that by reading the Bible we could both get to know God better before we went to see Him, whenever that was (since we all stand before God one day, when our life here is over). He thought that made sense. So we decided to begin meeting immediately to read the Bible together.

I stopped by to see him often (3 to 4 times a week) because I didn't know how much time he had left and I wanted him to have a true faith in Jesus. But after a month or so there was a problem. **There was an outbreak of bedbugs in Jimmy's apartment complex.** We thought there might be bedbugs in his apartment, but we weren't sure. One thing I was sure about – I didn't want to bring them into my house. I knew God sent me to Jimmy for a reason and I knew I would continue to go over after work, but this was still a problem for me. I've never had bedbugs in my house before, but I've helped several friends "debug" their homes. It's an extremely long, hard process.

So, I came up with an idea. I put a complete change of old clothes in my car. Before I went to see Jimmy, I changed into these clothes and then changed back into my work clothes as soon as I got home. Then my wife took the clothes that might have bedbugs in them and washed them immediately. This may seem a bit extreme but it seemed like a good solution to the problem. It allowed me to see Jimmy often, while reducing the risk of bringing the bugs home with me.

I still remember the many times I left Jimmy's apartment, scratching as I drove home. If you've ever been exposed to bedbugs, you know how you start to imagine that every small itch you have is probably bugs crawling on you. In spite of this, I really looked forward to my frequent visits with Jimmy.

Sometimes we talked for a long time. Sometimes we only talked for a few minutes because he was so ill and so tired. We talked about a lot of things. We talked about his life and his past. We watched TV together. We read the Bible together and

A BURRO FOR JESUS

we talked about Jesus. We talked about how this life is short for all of us compared to eternity. **We talked about the difference it makes to have a faith in Jesus – the difference it makes during our life here on Earth and during the life after this one.**

During this time, I asked a local pastor to stop by to talk with Jimmy as often as he could, since he lived nearby. Within six months or so, it became more difficult for me to see Jimmy as often as I wanted – due to my travel schedule and a few health issues I was having at the time. So the pastor saw Jimmy more often than I did. Within a year, he told me that Jimmy had become a believer in Jesus. Then, a little while after that, Jimmy died and went to see Jesus. Isn't it just like God to initially reach out to Jimmy through me and then provide someone else when needed?

Thank you, God, for sending us to Jimmy to tell him about your love for him. Every life is important to you. You tell us to gently instruct those who oppose the truth. Perhaps their hearts will change and they will learn the truth *(2 Timothy 2:25-26)*. You see the people who need to be rescued by You. Please send me to more of them and I'll tell them about Your love for them. I'm ready.

❦❦❦❦❦❦❦❦❦❦❦❦❦❦❦❦❦

We have a God who sends us to those who are hurting and in need of a personal touch from Him. What an honor to be asked by the creator of the universe to go to others as His ambassador!

When He asks us to go . . . let's go!

Chapter 19

Mike

. . . anyone who belongs to Christ has become a new person.
The old life is gone; a new life has begun!
2 Corinthians 5:17

Of all the people God has ministered to through me, no one person has impacted my life as much as Mike. I'm so glad God put Mike in my life.

I met his two kids a year or so before I met him, when they were both in high school. They were a part of my church's high school ministry, where I served as a volunteer. During this time, I came into contact with hundreds of high school students. There's something special about kids at this age. They have a refreshing enthusiasm for life and they're beginning to think more seriously about life and ask important questions – about relationships, about God and about other decisions they're facing.

For some reason, I was especially drawn to Mike's son and daughter when they joined the small group of students I met with every week. **I knew from my conversations with them that their dad was an alcoholic and an atheist.** Although their home life was difficult, they excelled in school – him in music and her in academics. As I spent time with them, I could see that they had a very close brotherly-sisterly bond with each other, perhaps a result of supporting each other through years of their father's drinking problem. I cared about all the kids in the church ministry, but I had a special place in my heart for these two.

One day it occurred to me – if I really cared about Mike's children, I would care about him too. So, after discussing it with them, I called Mike and asked if I could stop by to meet him. I was a bit nervous as I drove to his house for the first time. I wasn't sure what I'd say to him. I was also a little anxious about how he would respond to me. **Would he think that this "church guy" was coming over to "preach" to him or "judge" him.** I hoped not. I was expecting to have a brief, casual conversation with him without discussing any major topics. After all, we had never met before. I didn't want to offend him – just talk for a while. I assumed I would probably only visit him a few times. Surely, he would gladly embrace the new life he could enjoy with Jesus. Then I'd move on to whatever God had for me next. That was my plan. But God...

When Mike opened the door, his first comment surprised me. "So I guess you're here to see why I don't come to church and why I drink so much." he said.

"Well," I replied, "I actually came over to meet you and talk about your children. But since you brought it up, why don't we talk about those things first."

So, our first conversation had begun. It was one of many visits and many discussions we would have over the next seven years or so. During this time, I stopped by to see Mike often. What he told me about his life broke my heart. As a child, he had been the victim of terrible abuse. Later, after several years of marriage, his wife died shortly after giving birth to their second child. Then he became disabled and was unable to work. He had experienced a very difficult life.

At first I didn't understand why Mike would sometimes say I could stop by to see him but then he wouldn't answer the door when I arrived. His daughter explained that it might be easier to see him toward the end of each month because he would be sober then. By that time, the money from his Social Security check would be gone and he wouldn't be able to buy any more beer until his next check arrived. I discovered she was right. Although I continued to stop by to see Mike throughout the month, there was a greater chance that he would be sober and willing to see me at the end of each month.

Sometimes when I stopped by to see Mike, he would be angry or sarcastic. Sometimes he would be drunk. But usually he was none of these. Most of the time, he was very pleasant to talk to, especially after we had continued to meet for a while and we got to know each other better. We often talked for hours. He told me about his life, his children and his other interests which included writing poetry, listening to music and watching movies. I told him about my life, my family and my God. Some of my favorite memories with Mike were the times we went to the movies. Of course there were also the frequent conversations about life and about God. This went on for years. We were friends – good friends.

One day, about 4 years after that first visit, Mike said, "I'm really glad you come over to see me because no one else does. But do we have to talk about God every time you stop by?"

"I'm sorry," I replied, "It's hard for me to talk for long without talking about Him because He's been the best part of my life for so long. Stop me if I talk about Him too often and I'll change the subject."

Then, one day after meeting for more than five years, Mike asked me to pray for him. He said, "You know I don't believe in God yet."

"I know."

"But I see how happy you are because of your belief in God and I want to find that happiness. Please pray for enlightenment."

"O.K. But what do you mean by enlightenment?"

"You know," Mike replied, "Enlightenment about God. I want to find what you have found in God."

So I prayed for Mike. Then I said, "God isn't hiding from

you. He wants you to find Him. I have an idea. Let's start reading the Bible together. I believe God will reveal Himself to you the same way He does to me – through the Bible. I don't have to convince you of who God is. He'll do that."

So, I went by to see Mike 3 to 4 times a week and we started reading in the Bible – the book of John. He asked a lot of really good questions about God during our talks. Then something happened after we had met a few times to read the Bible. As we met that day and talked a while, I couldn't remember where we had stopped reading the last time (because I was reading through the book of John with another friend, and he and I were in a different part of "John").

So I said, "Mike, I don't remember where we left off."

"We stopped after chapter 6," he said. "I hope you don't mind but I've been reading ahead. I'm in chapter 14 and I have a lot of questions."

It was exciting to see his eagerness to read the Bible and his sincerity as he was searching for answers about God. About this same time, I introduced Mike to a few of my friends who had, with God's help, overcome years of alcohol and/or drug abuse. One of them, Kenny, had once been part of a famous blue grass country band. He had also struggled for years with his abuse of alcohol and drugs. Then Kenny's life was transformed when he found a new life with Jesus. Now he is a Christian who spends his life serving God full-time in a way that has impacted many lives, including mine. He took a real interest in helping Mike. When I visited Mike, he would tell me about the times when Kenny stopped by and the two of them played guitar together. They both loved music and had both played the guitar for years. Kenny was a meaningful part of Mike discovering the truth about God's love for him.

I remember the day Mike became a believer in God and a follower of Jesus. I remember when he stopped his abuse of alcohol. I remember the day we were driving to see a movie and Mike said, "Isn't life good?" I remember the day he and I helped a man stranded on the roadside with car trouble (see next chapter).

Then there was the day when he asked to come to church with me for the first time. He wanted to come but he was concerned that he might be nervous while he was there and he might need a cigarette. He was afraid the people there wouldn't like it if they saw him smoking. Even though I assured him that no one would object if he smoked outside the building, he wasn't so sure. I told him that I knew the people there and I was certain they wouldn't say anything. I also told him that if anyone did say something to him that I'd smoke a cigarette with him (although I didn't smoke). As I expected, no one said anything about his smoking. They accepted and loved Mike and were happy he was at church with them. Mike and I continued to meet regularly after that first time he came to church. He loved church, especially Pastor Rick's preaching.

Gradually, Mike's health grew worse. After fighting emphysema for years, Mike suddenly became very sick and was put into a hospice facility. Then came the day when his kids called me to say that it looked like he wouldn't make it through the day. I rushed over immediately with my daughter Jennifer and good friend Julie. Mike was unconscious when we arrived. As we all sat near him in his room, we shared memories of our times with him. Then his two children began to tell some of Mike's favorite jokes. The five of us shared a special time – as we all sat around laughing and lovingly reminiscing about our memories with Mike. Then we watched as his breathing slowed and he took his last breath.

What an ending for Mike – he died peacefully, surrounded by the people who loved him most. The sarcastic, angry man I met years before had become happy and contented. He had become a new man, one who had finally found peace, because of his seeking and finding God. Several months before Mike died, we were talking about our friendship over the prior seven years or so. **As we talked, he told me how much he hated me the first time he met me.** He said he hated me because he hated God and he hated the church – and I was a part of the church.

Over the years, I witnessed such a wonderful transformation in Mike's life, especially the last year or two. God replaced the hate in Mike's life with love. God took away Mike's addiction to alcohol. God changed Mike's life. God gave Mike a home in Heaven for all of eternity.

God gave me a good friend – my friend Mike. I'm so glad God put Mike in my life. I'm so glad God put others from my church into Mike's life, as he was on his journey to find God. I learned a lot about God during my years with Mike. I learned that God wants us to truly love our neighbors and invest ourselves into their lives, not just tell them about Jesus and move on.

God, thank you for my good friend Mike. Thank you for my best friend Jesus.

ꙮꙮꙮꙮꙮꙮꙮꙮꙮꙮꙮꙮꙮꙮꙮ

If you want to show your love for someone . . .
spend time with them.

Chapter 20

Chuck

. . . there is more joy in heaven over one lost sinner
who repents and returns to God than over ninety-nine others
who are righteous and haven't strayed away!
Luke 15:7

One day while I was in my office, I got a call from the receptionist. Someone was in the front lobby to see me. I was surprised because I didn't have an appointment on my schedule for that time. As I walked to the front desk, I was concerned that maybe I had scheduled an appointment and just forgotten to write it down.

When I got to the front desk, I didn't recognize the man who was there to see me. "I'm sorry," I said, "I wasn't expecting anyone. Did we have an appointment scheduled for today?"

"No," he said, "but I was in town and wanted to see you. Don't you recognize me?"

"I'm sorry, I don't," I replied. "What's your name?"

"I won't tell you. Think about it. Are you sure you don't recognize me?"

Then I remembered who he was. It was Chuck. I met him a year or two earlier when he was standing on the side of the road holding a sign asking for help. At the time, he was traveling from California to Florida with his girlfriend and their child. They were moving back to Florida to be closer to family, but they had broken down on their way there. Their van needed a water pump and they didn't have enough money to buy one. They were stranded. I was headed to a movie with my friend Mike (prior chapter) when we spotted Chuck. When we stopped to help, Mike surprised me by saying that he wanted to help me buy the water pump. Mike had a limited income, so his offering to help a stranger was one of those moments that continued to show me how Mike was changing, as he was learning more and more about God and God's desire for us to help others.

We gave Chuck the money he needed to fix his van and asked if he needed anything else. He said he wanted to stay in town for a while but didn't have enough money to rent a place. So, I made a call and several local churches took turns allowing all three of them to stay at their facilities (rent-free) for a while.

Then, Chuck began looking for a job in an effort to save the money needed for his trip home. He did work part-time at a few places but never found a full time job, so we made sure the three of them had the food and other necessities they needed. After several months, he had very little money saved but he still wanted to get to Florida as soon as possible. So, I gave him the money he needed for the trip and said goodbye as they drove away. I asked Chuck to let me know when he got to Florida safely and to call me occasionally to let me know how they were doing. He did call once, but he didn't stay in touch with me after that.

But now, here he was in my office more than a year later. We decided to go somewhere to talk for a while. He said he was there to thank me for all we had done to help him and his family, and to ask for my forgiveness. He was making amends for things he had done wrong in the past. He told me that he had lied to me while we were helping him. He was still using drugs on a regular basis during the whole time he was accepting money from us. We thought we were helping them buy food and other necessities. Of course they did buy food, but they were also buying drugs.

It seems that after he got to Florida, things didn't go well for a while. But now everything was different, because he had

🔺 A BURRO FOR JESUS

devoted his life to God. He and his girlfriend got married and he was now a staff member at a church in Florida. He showed me the church brochure with his picture in it. In fact, he had returned to my town recently to help a local ministry for a while.

He was now ministering to others who were trying to stop their abuse of alcohol or drugs. He was using his past and his faith in Jesus to help others. I was thrilled that Chuck now had a close walk with God and that God had used me and others I've never met to be a part of Chuck's story. Now Chuck was reaching out to others to tell them about the new life God promises to everyone through their faith in Jesus.

The things we did to help Chuck's seems small compared to how God is now working through Chuck's life. What an amazing story of how God takes the little we have to offer and uses it for something extraordinary. It reminds me of the day the little boy gave his 2 fishes and 5 loaves of bread to Jesus. As you may remember, Jesus gave thanks to His Heavenly Father for them and God multiplied the food – feeding more than 5,000 people (John, chapter 6). Jesus still takes what we offer to Him (our time, talents and resources) and uses it to bless others and glorify our Heavenly Father.

꧁꧂꧁꧂꧁꧂꧁꧂꧁꧂꧁꧂꧁꧂

We serve an amazing God! Let's serve Him well, with enthusiasm. Nothing we do for our Lord is done in vain (even when we don't see the results) . . . Absolutely nothing!
(1 Corinthians 15:58 - paraphrased)

Chapter 21

Danger

For He will order His angels to protect you wherever you go.
Psalm 91:11

It was late at night and I was at home watching TV. All of a sudden, I had a definite impression that I thought might be coming from God. I felt deep inside that He was trying to tell me,

"Your daughter is in danger . . . Pray for her."

Although it seemed like this thought might be coming from God, I ignored it initially. I thought maybe it was my imagination. This was not a normal occurrence.

But as the thought continued and became more urgent, I knew it had to be from God...

"Your daughter is in danger. Pray for her."

So, I turned off the TV and prayed for my daughter, Jennifer. After a few minutes, the feeling disappeared. So I thanked God for whatever He was doing to protect her and I stopped praying. I glanced at my watch. I wanted to remember the exact time that this had happened because I planned to ask Jennifer later if anything unusual had occurred that evening. This was in the days before cell phones, so I couldn't call her immediately to ask how she was doing.

I knew that she was driving home that night from a vacation in California with three of her friends. We didn't expect them to arrive home for several hours, so I went to sleep. When I saw her the next day, I asked her if anything had happened on her way home. I didn't say anything about God telling me to pray for her.

She said, "Yes, something did happen while Kelly was driving. It was late at night and dark and Kelly was driving through some mountains. I was in the back seat while the other two were sleeping. There was a moment when I noticed the headlights of our car shining on the side of the mountains. It appeared to be a white shape with two wings. Even though I knew it was just car lights reflecting off a dark mountain side, I remember thinking at the time how it looked like an angel and also thinking about how God is always with us."

"When we were out of the mountains," she continued, "Kelly told me what had happened to her. She said that she had suddenly become very sleepy while she was driving. At the time, there was no place to pull safely off the road. She said she became extremely worried as she continued to drive on the winding road with cars coming toward her while she was struggling to stay awake. **As her fatigue and her fear grew and she was close to panic, she was suddenly wide awake and her fear was gone.** After she told me about all that had happened to her, I told her about what I had seen. We finished the trip home with Kelly having no more difficulty staying awake as she drove."

I asked Jennifer what time this happened. You guessed it – It was the same time God asked me to pray for her the night before! After she finished her story, I told her about what I had experienced at the same time!

Years later, Jennifer and I were leading our group of cars to Mexico for a weekend mission trip. She was driving one of the cars and I was driving my truck. Her car was somewhere ahead of me but I couldn't see it.

All of a sudden I again felt that God was trying to tell me, **"Your daughter is in trouble. Pray for her."**

So I did. Later that evening, she told me that she had almost been hit head-on by a car. She said that while she was driving, there was a moment when she felt that she should slow down. Although it didn't make sense to her at the time, the feeling was so strong that she did slow down. About that same time, there was a line of cars approaching her from the other direction.

All of a sudden, one of them pulled out to pass another car. The driver of the car had misjudged the distance needed to pass and was headed directly toward my daughter – in her lane. Somehow at the last minute the car pulled back into its lane, barely avoiding a head-on collision with my daughter. She felt sure she might have been hit by the car if she had not felt the urge to slow down just before the car pulled out in front of her. When I asked her when this happened, I realized that it was about the same time God prompted me to pray for her.

Then, just last week, as I am writing this, it happened again - but this time it involved my son Stephen. As I was driving out of town early one morning, I was praying for my wife and children. While I prayed for Stephen, I sensed God telling me that Satan would like to end my son's life to end the ministry God was doing through him. **So I asked God to protect Stephen's life.** I remember feeling silly at the time to be praying such a strange prayer for someone who was only in his 30's and so healthy.

Two days later, my son told me what had happened to him as he was swimming in the ocean on the day I prayed for him. Listen as he describes it in his own words:

"I was snorkeling and spearfishing in the ocean. I shot a fish and came up to show my kids who were on the shore. But when I surfaced, the shore was further away than I thought and the current was taking me out even further. As I began to swim in, I suddenly got a cramp in my leg. No big deal, I thought, but as I kicked harder with the other leg, it began to cramp also."

"I tried to post up on the spear but the water was deeper than I expected and I went under. I knew I was drowning so I fought to get back to the surface and I began yelling – a yell like I have never yelled before. A fear-filled yell – **HELP!**"

"I saw my friend Gail start running toward the water to help, but I didn't think she would get there in time before I drowned. I kicked my legs hard to try and keep my head above the water, then I cramped and sank again."

Stephen later told me that he thought for sure that he was going to die. His next thought was about how bad this was going to be for his wife and children because they were going to watch him die as they stood on the shore and they would have that memory for the rest of their lives.

He was not aware of it at the time, but as he screamed out, there were 2 young men who were swimming nearby at this same time. They later said that they shouldn't have been there because their mother had planned for them to leave the beach and head home before all of this happened. But they had asked her for permission to go swimming before they left. As it turned out, they were both lifeguards and accomplished swimmers. They heard my son's screams for help and immediately swam to help. Fortunately, they just happened to be swimming close enough to reach Stephen in time. Gail continued to swim out until she reached them and the three of them helped Stephen get safely to shore.

Stephen told me he was surprised how long it took to swim against the current and make it to shore, even with all of them working together. He is certain that there was no way he would have survived if these men had not been close by, because he feels sure that he was too far out for Gail to reach him in time. If the two men had left earlier, as their mother had planned, this would have probably ended very badly.

I don't know a lot about all the things God does to protect us. **I also don't understand why He acts when we pray. But He does.** Sometimes His answers are exactly what we ask for. Sometimes they are different (yet better for us) because He knows what is best for us.

❦❦❦❦❦❦❦❦❦❦❦❦❦❦❦❦

When you feel prompted by God to pray for someone . . . do it.

A BURRO FOR JESUS

Chapter 22

Sleeping Bags

Suppose a brother or sister is without clothes and daily food.
If one of you says to them, "Go in peace; keep warm and well fed,"
but does nothing about their physical needs, what good is it?
James 2:15-16 (NIV)

For years I lived in a part of Arizona that is known for hot summers and mild winters. One year, we were hit with an extremely harsh cold front. When I woke up that Sunday, the temperature was below freezing and I thought about how hard it must be for the homeless people in our city. I was very concerned about how they could survive weather like this.

I had an idea. So, I went to church early and when I got there, I asked my pastor if he would make an announcement during the services that morning. I wanted people to meet me at the church later that day with sleeping bags, then join me as we took them to the homeless. He thought that was a good idea, so he made the announcement in both services.

People did show up that afternoon – about 10 of them with more than 60 sleeping bags! I was thrilled. One entire family came to help. The parents were so excited that their young children could be a part of helping people who were less fortunate. We weren't terribly organized, but we saw a need and we wanted to help. In fact, I wasn't even sure where to find the people who were homeless. This was before I joined the ministry to the homeless mentioned in chapter 27. Fortunately, someone in our group knew where many of the city's street people stayed at night. So off we went.

It was a memorable afternoon and evening as God's people reached out to help others in need. One specific moment stands out in my memory from that evening. It was when I watched one of the homeless men talking for a long time to one of the men from our group. The homeless man had no way of knowing that he was talking to the president of a very large and well-known international Christian ministry. This man didn't live in our city. In fact he lived in another country. He is a very humble man who loves Jesus a lot and he happened to be in the U.S. that day. He had been in our church service that morning and when he heard the announcement about taking sleeping bags to the homeless, he wanted to join us. Because of his position, he is a man who occasionally deals with leaders of other international ministries, as well as men who were the political leaders of their countries. But on this day, he wasn't talking to a Prime Minister or the king of a foreign country. He was leaning against the hood of a car earnestly listening to a homeless man tell his story. Watching this well-respected Christian leader talk for so long with a man who was down on his luck, really impressed me. He knew that God considers everyone, that God considers everyone to be precious and valuable, even those the world values very little.

Then several years later, we got snow again in Phoenix. When I got home from work, I got a call from a good friend of mine named Stan. Stan really loves Jesus. He was concerned about how the homeless people would stay warm that night. He suggested we get some sleeping bags and pass them out. So, a few of us went out that night to hand out sleeping bags and food to people we found sleeping on the streets. It was only sleeping bags (and socks and hats) that we gave to a few people, but to those men and women, it was warmth on a very cold night, because God cared enough to send someone to help them.

❀❀❀❀❀❀❀❀❀❀❀❀❀❀❀❀❀

God cares about everyone. When God gives you the opportunity to help someone – don't hesitate!

🔺 A BURRO FOR JESUS

Chapter 23

Len

Therefore, my dear brothers and sisters, stand firm.
Let nothing move you. Always give yourselves
fully to the work of the Lord, because you know that
your labor in the Lord is not in vain.
1 Corinthians 15:58 (NIV)

One of my favorite things to do is to go to a restaurant for an hour or two as often as I can to enjoy some quiet time with God and my Bible. One day, as I pulled into a restaurant parking lot, I was approached by a young man I didn't know. His name was Len. He said that he had no money and his truck was almost out of gas. I thought, because of his appearance, that he might be homeless and that he might need more than fuel for his truck. But when I asked if he had a place to stay, he said he did have somewhere to live. He also said he had a job, but on that particular day he had no money and wasn't sure he had enough gas to get home.

I didn't know if he was telling the truth about everything but I told him I would put a little gas in his truck if he'd follow me to the gas station across the street. While we were there, we only had a few minutes to talk so I asked him a few questions about himself. I also shared several brief thoughts with him about God. Before he left, I gave him my telephone number and told him to call me if I could ever be of help to him.

I didn't hear from Len for several months. Then, one night he called me while I was eating pizza with my family at a local restaurant. **He said he had lost his job and he was now homeless and living in his truck.** So, I drove to where he was, took him to a fast food restaurant and we talked for a while as he ate. He said he had been looking for work with no success and wondered if I knew anyone who was hiring. I told him I didn't know of any jobs available at that time but I would pray about it and check around. We prayed together and I gave him a sleeping bag to help him stay warm that evening.

Then, I invited him to join me at a men's Bible study at 6:30 the next morning. I don't think I would have thought to ask him to come to our Bible study if it had not been for my oldest son, James. He was with me the night I got the call from Len. When he heard that Len was looking for work, he said he had heard that the economy was good in Texas and there might be work there. It was kind of a random idea from him – that there might be work in Texas. We lived in Arizona and didn't know anyone in Texas.

I knew the Bible study that I'd be attending the next morning with my son, Stephen, was led by a man who used to live in Texas. I thought maybe he would know of someone there who could offer a job to Len. So, that's the primary reason I asked Len to join us. Actually, as it turned out, God wanted him to be there for another reason.

While at the Bible study, one of the men in the group (Nate) heard from my son that Len was homeless. To my surprise, he came up to us after the Bible study to offer his help to Len. He invited him to live at his house until he could find a job and save up enough money to get a place of his own. Even though Nate would be at work all day, he gave Len a key to his house so he would have a place to stay that day. I asked Nate privately if he was sure that he wanted to do that. I told him I had only met Len recently and didn't know him very well.

But Nate wanted to help, so he gave a key to Len. Nate then made several phone calls and arranged a job interview for Len in a few days. Nate also bought him a cell phone to help as he looked for a job. One of the other men in the Bible study told some friends at his church about Len's need for clothes and they gladly became a part of the group who wanted to help Len get back on his feet.

Isn't it great how God's people are used by Him to reach out to people in need? I am often thrilled as I witness the generosity and compassion shown by God's people to those who need help. We can spot true disciples of Jesus by the love they show for each other and to those around them.

I wish I could tell you that this part of the story had a happy ending, but it didn't. Len stayed at Nate's house for a few days but decided not to show up for the job interview that Nate set up for him. It became obvious that he had a drinking problem. Then Len left. I don't know where he is today. But I know my God. He asks us to share His love with those around us by helping people when they are in need. We are to lovingly speak the truth to them, while not enabling them to continue a life of bad decisions. Then, He tells us that He is responsible for the results, not us. We are only responsible to obey Him and love others.

I have no doubt that God will send others to Len to point him back to Jesus and the life he can have with God – a life of purpose and meaning. I trust God will do this because He has heard our prayers and He wants Len to enjoy a personal relationship with Him.

🌿🌿🌿🌿🌿🌿🌿🌿🌿🌿🌿🌿🌿🌿

As you read this, please pray for Len.

Chapter 24

Thailand Concert

. . . may He equip you with all you need for doing His will
Hebrews 13:21

In 2004, a tsunami hit Thailand. The loss of life and the property damage there was massive and tragic. After hearing about the tsunami, a small group from our church felt that God wanted them to go there to help.

We didn't want to rush over there without a real plan. We could possibly interfere with the ongoing relief efforts being provided by so many from around the world who went to Thailand to help. So, we contacted Kelly, one of our good friends who worked for a Christian relief organization located in Thailand, to offer our help. Initially, we were told that the country of Thailand was closed to any more outside groups coming over to offer assistance.

Although we felt God was leading us to go to Thailand, we checked into the possibility of going to other countries that were also hit by the tsunami. We continued to pray about what God wanted us to do, and before long we received a call from Kelly.

She said, "Guess what? We are now able to accept teams in Thailand, and yours will be one of the first to come!"

We were so excited! Our group couldn't leave for a while because it would take a few months to get the required immunization shots and to raise the money needed for the trip. During this time, we planned for the trip and we all met every week to pray about the trip. **This was such a sweet time of prayer – a small group of people pouring out their hearts to God for hours each week and asking for His direction and His help.**

I still think about those months of prayer. We met every Wednesday night around 8:00 p.m. What I remember most is how often our group prayer time was nothing but silence. No one needed to talk as we each individually enjoyed the presence of our Lord. It reminds me of one of my favorite Bible passages about prayer – *Ecclesiastes 5:2, "Don't make rash promises, and don't be hasty in bringing matters before God. After all, God is in heaven and you are here on earth. So let your words be few."*

As the time for the trip approached, there was a problem. Most of the money we needed had still not been raised. We were about $11,000 short of funding the expenses of the trip. We weren't overly concerned because we had organized a special concert that we thought would raise the money we needed. But the earliest we could schedule the concert was a week or so after the group was scheduled to go to Thailand. To help our efforts, someone loaned us the money we needed for the trip with our promise that we would pay it back after we raised the funds ourselves. We realized that it is usually better to raise the money needed before the trip than after. But we felt God wanted us to go and we believed that God would provide the funding, so my daughter and the others in the group left for Thailand. I was not part of the group going to Thailand. I stayed behind and helped with the details of the concert.

The concert itself was different than anything we had ever done before. Through the efforts of one of the ladies in our group, two well-known musicians agreed to fly in at their own expense to perform at our "Thailand concert". One of them was a popular musician in California. The other one was the lead singer of a very successful Christian band (whose music was played often on Christian radio stations around the country).

We were thrilled that two men who were so well known had heard about our trip and agreed to help us raise funds. We decided we wouldn't charge admission for the concert. During

A BURRO FOR JESUS

the concert we would ask for donations. To promote the event, we passed out thousands of flyers in our area and had announcements made on local Christian radio stations.

We were expecting a big turnout, so we scheduled 2 concerts (Friday and Saturday night) at a very large church. I had decided to not use my church because it only seated about 600 people. We had a lot of volunteers scheduled to come on both nights to help us handle the details of what I expected to be a very crowded event.

So we were ready. The citywide advertising campaign was done. The two musicians arrived into town. The church auditorium was reserved, and the volunteers were ready. All we needed was for the crowd to show up. Our goals for the concert were to glorify God through this event, raise the $11,000 needed, and to see people give their lives to Jesus as a result of the gospel message that would be shared during the concert.

Friday night arrived and only 11 people showed up for the concert! Really, only 11 (we counted them)! Guess what happened on Saturday? Again only 11 people showed up! Exactly 11 just like Friday night! Of the eleven people who came on Saturday, one was a well-known local professional sports star and two were a homeless couple who saw the cars outside the church and came in hoping to get some food. We had almost as many volunteer workers at each event as concert goers!

What did we do? All of us agreed – we were there to glorify God, so the two musicians did a full concert each night for the handful of people who attended. **One little boy brought in a container full of coins and bills he had been saving ever since he saw the pictures of the tsunami on TV.** He donated a little more than $38. It was touching to see the compassion and the generosity of this young boy to help people overseas who he didn't even know. When the offering was counted, we couldn't believe it. A little over $10,000 was donated the first night and another $500 or so on the second night! The remaining money came in quickly from other sources. So we paid back the money that had been loaned to us.

Oh! Remember the homeless couple who came to the second concert? After the show was over, my friend Derek and I took them to get something to eat. While we were there, we told them about Jesus and the joyful life that He offers to all of us. The woman was already a Christian. She had decided to follow Jesus years before. The man listened and decided that night to give his life to Jesus and to become a Christian.

It was a concert to remember! Only 22 people showed up, but . . . God had been glorified and almost all the money we needed was raised, and a homeless man decided to follow Jesus and join the family of God! Shortly after the concert, our group returned from Thailand with many stories about how they had been used by God.

🌱🌱🌱🌱🌱🌱🌱🌱🌱🌱🌱🌱🌱

When God directs you to go somewhere for Him . . . Go. He will provide!

Chapter 25

Sitting Alone

Think about the things of heaven, not the things of earth.
Colossians 3:2

One day, I called my wife and asked her if she wanted to go to a movie and then out for dinner. Since we were in different parts of town at the time, we decided to drive separately and meet at the theater.

I don't remember what movie we saw that day, but I remember what happened at the restaurant. As we sat and enjoyed our dinner together, a woman who was sitting alone at a nearby table kept talking to us. She talked mostly about the weather and about politics. More specifically, she was complaining about how hot it was and how bad things were in our country because of our politicians. She was very nice, but her conversation was mostly negative, with a word or two of profanity sprinkled throughout.

After a while, I assumed the reason she was sitting next to us and continuing to talk to us was because God wanted me to talk to her about Jesus. **I don't know about you, but sometimes when I see people sitting alone at a restaurant, I assume they are there alone because God wants me to talk to them about Jesus.** After my wife and I finished our dinner, I told her we had an opportunity to stay and talk with our new friend about God. So, I asked the woman if we would be intruding if we joined her at her table for a few minutes.

When she invited us to sit, I said, "You have been so nice to my wife and I and we may never see each other again . . .

so I wondered if I could ask you something?"

"Sure," She said.

"Many years ago someone told me that the way to be happy for my entire life was to get to know God personally. So I did and He's been the best part of my life ever since. I was wondering, is God a part of your life? Do you have a personal relationship with Him?"

She told me that she had not attended church since she was very young. Although she had made a decision back then to follow Jesus, she had turned away from Him and had not included God in her life for many years.

We talked for a few minutes, then she asked, "Can I tell you some of my favorite Bible verses from when I was a child?"

It was a wonderful time as we took turns sharing some of our favorite verses. Then we talked about God for a while and I encouraged her to find a good church to attend that would help her develop a close walk with our God.

I don't remember her name or what she looked like. As far as I know, she made no major decisions about Jesus that night. We didn't discuss any deep theological principles. **But I felt the time was precious because for a little while we stopped talking about politics and the weather and talked about Jesus.** He is so worthy of our thoughts and our conversation – all the time.

The Bible says we should look for ways to please our God *(Ephesians 5:10)*. God, I hope You were pleased as You listened to us talk about You that evening. I'm sure pleased with You…all the time.

❀❀❀❀❀❀❀❀❀❀❀❀❀❀❀❀❀

May I encourage you, as you read this . . . direct more and more of your thoughts and your conversation to be about our Lord . . . He is worthy!

🔺 A BURRO FOR JESUS

Chapter 26

A Call From a Client

But whenever someone turns to the Lord, the veil is taken away.
2 Corinthians 3:16 (NIV)

One day when I was at my office, I got a call from a client. He said he had just been released from the hospital and had been told by the doctors that he wasn't expected to live much longer. He asked if I could come over to make sure his estate was in order before he passed away. Although most of our conversations over the years were about his investments that I helped manage for him, I had mentioned God's name to him several times in the past. From his responses I assumed he was a Christian, but I had never asked him specifically if he knew God personally and if he knew for certain that he was going to Heaven after he died.

Now, I was concerned whether he had a personal relationship with God or not. So, I canceled all my appointments for the day and hurried over to see him. When I got there I could tell that he was very ill. As he sat there, he had tubes running from an oxygen tank to his nose to help him breathe.

It was obvious, as we talked briefly about his medical condition, that he was very weak, so I got right to the point. I asked him if he was a Christian and if he knew for sure he was going to Heaven after he died. He said he didn't know for sure what would happen after he died. In fact, he didn't think it was possible to know for sure. I assured him that there was a way he could know beyond any doubt. Then I asked him his opinion of Jesus. **He said he wasn't sure who Jesus was and that he had never really bought into the whole church and religion thing.** I told him that Jesus didn't like religion either, but Jesus loved him very much.

I began to tell him my story about how I came to know Jesus personally, and how he could do the same. As I began to explain the full gospel message to him, I could tell that he really didn't understand what I was trying to tell him. Quite honestly, as I listened to what I said, it didn't make a lot of sense to me either. I thought to myself – "I've told a lot people the good news about Jesus over the years. Why am I having so much trouble explaining it today? I know I can do better than this, but I'm not."

So, I pulled a gospel tract out of my back pocket and I read it to him. Then we talked for a while and I answered questions he had about God. He said that some of his friends had told him about Jesus years ago but it never seemed to make a lot of sense to him. Now, as we continued to talk, he was beginning to understand. After a while, he said he wanted to ask Jesus to become a part of his life. So we prayed together and talked for a while longer. Although we were having a really good conversation about God, I could see that he was very tired, so I left with a promise that I would return to talk with him again. By the way, we did take care of his estate issues quickly before I left. I visited with him several times and we talked about his new faith in Jesus, before he passed away and went to be with God.

God, Thank You for sending me to talk to my friend. Thank You for offering eternal life in Heaven to all who decide to believe in and follow Jesus. *You loved all of us so much that You gave Your one and only son, that whoever believes in Him shall have eternal life. (John 3:16 -KJV)*

❧❧❧❧❧❧❧❧❧❧❧❧❧❧❧

Chapter 36 has a more detailed explanation of the joy and peace we find when we know God personally and Jesus becomes our best friend.

Chapter 27

Homeless

Shout with joy to the Lord, all the earth! Worship the Lord with gladness. Come before Him, singing with joy. Acknowledge that the Lord is God! He made us, and we are His. We are His people, the sheep of His pasture. Enter His gates with thanksgiving; go into His courts with praise. Give thanks to Him and praise His name. For the Lord is good. His unfailing love continues forever, and His faithfulness continues to each generation.
(Psalm 100)

I was recently talking to a homeless friend of mine. She had worked her entire adult life until she became disabled, then eventually lost her home and ended up living on the streets. Here's a part of what she said,

"When I was working and had a home, I thought homeless people were lazy, that they didn't want to work. I never thought I would be homeless. Then I had an accident and couldn't work anymore. I began receiving disability income but I became homeless after I lost my home. It was scary, especially at night. You have to learn how to survive when you're homeless. It's hard to be homeless. You have to watch out for robbers and always be on your guard for your safety."

The friend mentioned above is one of many homeless people I've known. For a number of years, I helped my good friend Julie and my daughter Jennifer in their ministry to feed people who were homeless in downtown Phoenix. Julie's idea was that we would provide a warm home-cooked meal every Tuesday night to people who lived on the streets, then we would stay with them for an hour or two to talk with them and listen to their stories.

We wanted to share God's love for them through our words and actions. It was our hope that we could develop meaningful relationships with them and offer our help to those who wanted to get off the street. The first week, Julie cooked a pan of enchiladas and a few of us went downtown to look for people who were homeless. We served food and beverages to about a dozen people. The ministry had started. Within a few years, we were serving more than 100 people every week and had been joined by about a dozen volunteers who wanted to help minister to the poor and the homeless.

I have so many good memories of those times with our homeless friends. Some memories aren't quite as good – there were the two guys who tried to stab me with a knife, the one who tried to stab Julie and the one who did stab one of the homeless men attending our dinner. But these moments were rare. The moments that were plentiful were all the good conversations with our new friends and the times we were able to help them in very real ways. Let me tell you about two of my homeless friends – Jimmy and Bill.

Before we served the meal to the homeless each week, one of us would share a short devotional message from the Bible with them. One night, as I was sharing from the Bible, one of the homeless men named Jimmy shouted out, "I serve Satan."

Later that evening, as he and I sat on the curb together, I told him, "You and I both know that you don't serve Satan. You just wanted some attention tonight. I wouldn't shout out like that while you were speaking, so please don't do it again." Then I added, "You know God is pursuing you, don't you? He wants you in His family. Why don't you give your life to Him tonight?"

"Do I have to give up alcohol and drugs and women?" he asked.

"Yes," I replied.

"No," Jimmy said, "I don't want to give them up."

A little while after this, Jimmy disappeared for several months. We were all concerned about him. It was rarely good when one of our homeless friends disappeared. We didn't know where he was or if he was okay. None of his friends seemed to know where he was either.

Then one day, Jimmy called my daughter and told her that he had given his life to God and he had joined a rehab program. He had been sober and drug-free for six months. He said he was graduating that Sunday from the program and asked us if we would attend the ceremony. Of course we did. We were so proud of him as we watched him walk across the stage and receive his certificate.

Later, when I asked Jimmy how he came to God, I was surprised by what he told me. He said that one day he was sitting on the curb and he was so drunk he could barely move. Then some children on the other side of the street saw him and began throwing rocks at him. They saw he couldn't chase after them in his condition and they thought it was funny to throw rocks at him.

Jimmy said that as he sat there, he thought, "Life can't get much worse than this. I'm homeless, these kids are throwing rocks at me and I am so drunk I can hardly move." Just then a church bus pulled up in front of him.

When the door opened the bus driver said, "We're going to church. Want to come with us?"

Jimmy thought, "Why not?"

So he got on the bus. Then he joined the church's rehab program and God helped him clean up his life. After his graduation, he got a job and an apartment. Although he moved to a different part of town and didn't join us for a meal when we fed the people every week, I continued to meet with him occasionally to see if he was OK and help him with his new walk with Jesus.

Then there was Bill. He was homeless too. One night, after we had served the meal to everyone, he asked if I would meet with him later that week and talk for a while. I didn't know what he wanted to talk about but I knew several of us had offered to help him go back East to restore the relationship with his family.

So, we met a few days later for breakfast at a restaurant across from the library. As we talked, he pointed to the bushes on the side of the library and told me that he slept behind them at night. We talked for a long time, but not about anything specific. He just wanted to hang out together to talk – as friends do. While we were there, he asked if he could read his favorite part of the Bible to me. It was Psalm 100 – a psalm that gives praise and thanks to our Lord. Check it out in the Bible. **Isn't it amazing that this would be a homeless man's favorite part of the Bible?**

Sometime later, I got a call from Bill late one night. He had decided to go back home to reunite with his family. This would be the first step to him getting off the streets and beginning a new life. He said he was leaving that night and asked if I would drive downtown to see him before he left town. I assumed he had called because he needed money for the bus ticket to get home. But that was OK. I was delighted he was going home and would no longer be homeless. I was happy to buy the ticket for him. My wife and I weren't thrilled that I would be driving to a high crime part of town late at night. But I went, because seeing Bill was more important than staying home where I felt completely safe.

When I got there, we talked for a little while as it rained lightly. I offered to give him money for his ticket and for the food he would need during the trip. I also offered to drive him to the bus station. But he said he already had money for the ticket and for food and that he also had a ride to the station. He had called me because he wanted to say goodbye in person before he left. I was very touched that he valued our friendship

A BURRO FOR JESUS

that much. It's an evening I'll always remember. I asked him to call me occasionally to let me know how he was doing. I did get several calls from him within that year and he told me that he was doing good and his return home was going well.

As I write this, I haven't heard from Bill in several years. I hope he's still doing well. I did hear from Jimmy a few years ago. He was discouraged and thought it would be easier to go back to the homeless life he had known before. When he called, I was boarding an airplane to go out of town for a few days, so I asked him to meet with me when I returned so we could talk. But he never called me. I tried to call him but his phone had been disconnected. Apparently he did decide to turn away from God and return to the streets. It broke my heart.

But I know my God. He is not through with Jimmy yet. This was not the final chapter for Jimmy. God allowed me (and others in our group) to help Jimmy (and Bill) during this time in their lives. And I'm so glad He did. I'm sure He'll send someone else to help them during the rest of their lives. Because that's what He does. He's a God of love who pursues those He loves who are lost and wandering (often using us in His pursuit).

🐴🐴🐴🐴🐴🐴🐴🐴🐴🐴🐴🐴🐴🐴🐴🐴

I still pray for Jimmy and Bill . . . Would you please do the same?

Chapter 28

The Room

When God's people are in need, be ready to help them.
Always be eager to practice hospitality.
Romans 12:13

Several years ago, after the last of our 3 children moved away, my wife and I decided to downsize and move to a smaller home. We wanted to reduce our monthly expenses and no longer needed a larger house – at least that's what we thought. Our new home wasn't a lot smaller, but it was older, so it cost much less than the one we sold.

After a while, our daughter decided to move back home. We were delighted that she came back home to live with us. Then one of her friends needed a place to stay for a little over a year, so she stayed with us. When she moved out, another of my daughter's friends needed a place to stay, so she moved in for a while. Over about five years, four of my daughter's female friends from church and one of my good friends lived with us for as long as they wanted. My mother-in-law also stayed with us for the last year of her life as she was fighting cancer.

Fortunately, our house had a spare room. My wife and I were happy to freely offer this room to some of our family and friends who needed a place to live. Some stayed for only a month or so, some for more than a year. Except for my mother-in-law, none of the others who lived with us were relatives – they were just friends when they moved in. But after they were with us for a while, they became part of our family. Today we still think of them as part of our family – although they no longer live with us. Our efforts to downsize did not go according to plan. But God's plan was so much better. That room never seemed to stay empty for long. As a result, our family grew larger. How lucky we are.

Over the years, some of the people who stayed with my wife and I have talked to us about the time they lived with us. I specifically remember two conversations. I was a bit surprised when they said what a special time it was for them.

My response to each was about the same, "Stephanie and I didn't do anything special," I said, "just offered you a room to live in."

"It was more than that." they replied. "It was a haven. It was a home where we were accepted and loved, not judged. It was a safe place. We've never had that before."

Stephanie and I were so blessed as we opened up our home and our hearts to these friends who needed a place to stay for a while. By the way – my wife and I recently moved to a smaller house in another city and our friend Julie is renting the house from us that's mentioned above. She recently offered this same room to several people who have needed a place to stay rent-free (including the woman mentioned in chapter 32 titled "Help"). This room continues to be used in a way that honors God and helps people in need.

🌾🌾🌾🌾🌾🌾🌾🌾🌾🌾🌾🌾🌾🌾🌾

God blesses us all as we use what He gives us to help others! So let's give joyfully!

Chapter 29

Special Christmas

And don't forget to do good and to share with those in need.
These are the sacrifices that please God.
Hebrews 13:16

For years, Stephanie and I have enjoyed buying food and gifts for families who need help making Christmas special for their children. Several years ago, after helping some families in our neighborhood, she and I talked about wanting to help someone else. We didn't have a lot of extra money that year but we knew we had more than others. **We've discovered over the years that even though it is good to give to others out of our surplus, there seems to be something especially gratifying to give when we don't have a surplus.**

Then, we got a call from our friend, Julie. She heard about a family that would be homeless soon if someone didn't help. So, I called the telephone number that she gave me and went over immediately to meet them. I'm so glad I did.

When I got there, I met Penny and her four grandchildren. She was retired and taking care of her grandchildren because her daughter was in jail. One of the first things I noticed about Penny was how much she smiled and how happy she was, in spite of her situation. She had a love for God and an attitude about life that was contagious. As she spoke, her trust in God was obvious. I could see immediately that all of the children were well cared for and very polite.

As Penny and I sat down to talk, she told me that she had been accustomed to a comfortable income over the years. But now, through a series of events, she had lost their home and found herself in a motel room with the kids. She had recently taken the remaining money she had from her last Social Security check and prepaid the cost of the motel room for several days. It would be more than a week before she got her next check. She and the children would have to leave the motel just a few days before Christmas. They would soon have no home, no food and no Christmas gifts.

I knew we had to help, so I called Stephanie as I drove home and she jumped into action. My wife is an amazing person. She loves helping people and especially loves shopping for someone who has a special need. When I returned later that day to the motel room, I had food and a small Christmas tree with lights and decorations. We all had such a fun time as we decorated the tree and the room. It was no longer just a small motel room. **It was a home, filled with the glow and sparkle of Christmas.** As I'm writing this, I still remember the smiles on the faces of the little children. I told Penny that we wanted to bless them with Christmas presents, and asked her for some gift ideas. Later that day I gave Stephanie the "list" and within a few days, there were gifts under the tree. Now the kids had really big smiles – they could see and touch their gifts and dream with anticipation about Christmas morning.

They would be okay for the week of Christmas, but what about the last week of December before Penny's Social Security check arrived? My wife and I were delighted that God wanted us to help Penny, but we thought we might need a team to help with her ongoing needs. So, we decided to tell some of our friends about Penny and let them become a part of the blessing and joy we receive when we give to others. I called my church and asked if they would help. They didn't hesitate. With the money provided by them and a few of our friends, we were able to get another motel room and more food for Penny and her family. The new motel offered a special reduced rate for weekly tenants and had a kitchen so Penny could cook food for her family and not have to eat at fast food restaurants.

All of this provided a temporary solution until something more permanent could be done. Because of Penny's need to care for her grandchildren, she couldn't look for a job. But she proved to be very resourceful and worked hard to help herself. She never asked for anything specific and was always grateful for everything we did to help her. Within a few weeks, she found an apartment that was within her budget and close to a good school for her grandchildren. Her Social Security check would now cover their monthly expenses. She would not be homeless and her grandchildren would not enter the state system for homeless children!

As I look back now, I am so grateful that God brought Penny into our lives. Her family survived a very difficult time – due partly to our efforts but mostly due to Penny's faith in God. We are fortunate enough to be the ones God chose to send to Penny in her time of need.

Even though it has been a few years since the day I first met her, I continue to talk with Penny from time to time. She called a year or so after we first met to thank me again for our help and to let me know that they were all doing well. In fact, she had been saving her money and now had enough for a down payment. She and the children would soon be moving into their own house!

As I conclude this story, I remember a time many years ago when my wife and I needed help. Although I was working full-time, we were out of money. Due to our financial difficulties, we lost the house we were buying. Then, within about a year, there was a month when I could not make the monthly payment on the house we were renting. I didn't know what to do. As I came home from work late one night, I was met by a couple leaving our house. My wife and I only knew them as very casual acquaintances, so I didn't know why they would be at our house that late in the evening. We spoke briefly as we passed on the walkway and then they said goodbye and left. When I went inside, I couldn't believe what my wife told me. This couple heard about our situation and came over to our house with the money we needed to pay our rent and buy food for that month.

At the time of our need, God showed up. He provided for us through some of His people. I am so glad that God now chooses to use my wife and I to help others.

❦❦❦❦❦❦❦❦❦❦❦❦❦❦❦

We serve an amazing God!

Ask Him to send someone to you that needs help (physically or spiritually).

He'll do it.

Chapter 30

The Bus Station

When you go through deep waters, I will be with you.
When you go through rivers of difficulty, you will not drown.
When you walk through the fire of oppression, you will not be
burned up: the flames will not consume you.
Isaiah 43:2

It was quite a scene at the bus station parking lot that day. But I'll get to that later. First let me tell you about Tom. I initially met him at a burger place where my friend Jim and I were meeting to read the Bible. Jim and I invited him to join us for a burger. Tom had been going door to door asking for donations to help a home for veterans where he lived. Jim had met him several weeks before, when he stopped by Jim's house asking for a donation. Now here he was – at the same restaurant where Jim and I were meeting.

Over the next few months, Tom met with Jim and I several times and told us a lot about his life. He was proud of his American Indian heritage and was very skilled in making jewelry, using beautifully handcrafted polished gems. Tom told me in casual conversation that he was a veteran. I discovered later that he had once had a very distinguished military career. **In fact, he'd been involved in a key historical military event, as a member of the Special Forces.**

Now, many years later, Tom was divorced, facing several health issues and had not had a full time job for a while. **In spite of a difficult life that had resulted in being homeless occasionally, Tom was now a Christian and was optimistic about the future.** We became friends. He called me from time to time and we met occasionally to talk as friends do. He rarely asked for anything, but Jim and I would offer to help as we saw specific needs that he had.

One day, Tom asked me if he could join me at church. He seemed to enjoy it, although he only came that one time. A month or so later, Tom said he wanted to be baptized. So, on a very memorable day, a few of us gathered at a backyard pool and watched Tom declare his love for Jesus as he was baptized by Jim.

Then a few months later, Tom called and said he might soon be homeless again . . . right before Christmas! So Jim and I met with him and after discussing all of his options, we asked if he wanted to live with his family for a while until things got better for him. They lived in the eastern part of the country and he hadn't seen them for a while because his relationship with them hadn't been very good for years. He decided he wanted to return home and try to reconcile with them, but he didn't have enough money to make the cross country trip. So Jim and I offered to buy his bus ticket. The next day, Tom hopped in my car with the four bags he wanted to take on the bus. Jim loaded the rest of Tom's belongings into his truck and told Tom that he would store them at his house until Tom wanted them again.

When we got to the bus station, we were told that Tom's four bags exceeded the limit unless we wanted to pay for additional luggage. Unfortunately, we didn't have the extra money for that. I felt bad that he couldn't take everything with him, but it took almost all the money we had for his bus ticket.

So, there we were in the parking lot of the bus station as he unpacked all four bags to decide what to take with him. As I watched, I realized it was probably a strange sight to people walking by; they saw someone scattering his clothes and other belongings on the black asphalt surface as he packed all he could into two bags. But I saw something different. I saw a man who once had a successful military career and a promising future; but now, most of what he owned would fit into the bed of a pickup truck.

The storms of life had knocked him around for years, but he was still standing strong. In spite of getting more and more beat up by recent events, he remained optimistic and hopeful about the future. He was headed home and I would miss him. I enjoyed our time together.

As I stood there watching him in the parking lot, a thought occurred to me. Around the world there were a lot of people engaged in endeavors that were considered very important. But I thought no one had a more important job than Jim and I had that day. We had been chosen by the King of this universe, God himself, to help someone who is not valued much by the people of this world – but is greatly valued by God. Tom was, and is, a child of God, and God saw him in his despair. God allowed us to be the ones to go and help rescue him from a situation that was becoming desperate. **God saw Tom being battered by the storms of life and wanted him to know that he mattered and that he was not alone.**

As it turned out, Tom didn't stay with his family long because his efforts to reconcile with them didn't go well. He called me one day to tell me that he was walking and hitch-hiking back to Arizona. I offered to send money for a bus ticket, but he said he would come back on his own, carrying his things in a big back pack. He and I talked by phone several times as he was traveling across the country. He was in no hurry to get back to Arizona and he seemed to enjoy seeing the country-side and camping in the woods at night.

Tom is back in Arizona now, living with friends in another part of the state. I saw him a few years ago, when I got his remaining belongings from Jim and took them to Tom's new home. He still had no home of his own but was hopeful that he would qualify for government housing soon, as a result of his military background and his health issues. His life is still challenging, but Tom is very resourceful and optimistic, as he continues on life's journey – trusting God through life's ups and downs.

Do you feel beat up by the storms of life?
God sees you . . . talk to Him . . . you are not alone.
If you are the one God sends to help someone during a storm
of life – go to them and carry Jesus's love to them!

Chapter 31

Super Bowl Sunday

Jesus said, "Come to me, all you are weary and carry heavy burdens and I will give you rest."
Matthew 11:28

One day, I got a call from a pastor who asked if I would be the guest speaker at an upcoming event at his church. I thanked him for the invitation and told him I'd let him know my answer after I prayed about it. This was an unexpected and unusual invitation for me. In fact, I was very surprised by the offer. When people are looking for someone to speak at their church and they put together a list of their candidates, I'm not very high on the list – in fact, I'm usually not on the list at all. I'm not known for speaking to groups. Although I felt honored by the invitation, it didn't make a lot of sense to me. There were other people available who were more talented speakers than I was. But as I prayed about it, I felt like God wanted me to accept the invitation. So I did. **As we were to discover, God had a reason for me being there.**

On the day of the event, I felt in my spirit, as I was praying, that God was giving me a special message for someone in the group. Before I stood up to speak to everyone, I sensed the same thought from God again.

So, I began by saying . . . "Before I speak to you tonight, I feel God has a specific message for someone here tonight. I don't know who you are or what you are going through, but He knows. The message He has for you is: **. . . I see you . . . You are not alone . . . I see you as holy."**

Then I shared a message from the Bible. After I finished,

several people stayed behind and asked one of our leaders to pray with them about specific decisions they were making. One of the men waited until I was available to speak, and asked me to promise not to tell anyone about our conversation. Although I was surprised by his request, I agreed without giving it much thought. Then, I listened as he told me about a secret from his past. My heart broke for him as he told me about how he had been bullied and mistreated during his school years. For years he had lived with his memories of the past and the low self-esteem and pain it caused. We talked for a while and then we prayed together. He had not talked to anyone about this before that night. **He had carried this burden alone and it had become overwhelming to him.**

The next day was Sunday. In fact, it was Super Bowl Sunday. I love watching pro football. I especially love watching the Super Bowl. I had not missed watching a Super Bowl game in the past forty years or so. But, all I could think about that afternoon was what the man had shared with me. I wanted to talk with him again. He needed to find the peace and comfort that only God can give.

I knew I had promised to keep his secret. But I also knew this thing was destroying him and none of his family or friends could help him because they knew nothing about it. So, I contacted the pastor and asked if he knew where the man lived. He told me that the man's parents were members of his church and he gave me their address, so I went over immediately, hoping the man's parents would know where I could find their son.

When I rang the doorbell, his mother opened the door. I told her briefly who I was and said that I was looking for her son. I was in luck. It turned out that he was there to watch the Super Bowl later with his family. So, she invited me to come inside, then she introduced me to her husband and called for

A BURRO FOR JESUS

her son. When he entered the room, I could see that he was surprised and uneasy that I was there at his parent's house. He didn't want his secret revealed. I immediately brushed by his parents and asked him to come outside with me to talk. I realized later that I was so focused on his pain that I had skipped the usual formalities when meeting someone for the first time. I'm sure his parents may have wondered who this guy was who came into their house then immediately ignored them while he went outside to talk to their son, with no explanation to them.

Once we were outside, I tried to convince him to tell his parents about the secret he had been hiding, so they could help him. He said he couldn't. I told him that I was a parent and I was certain that his parents would want to know about something that was hurting him so badly. I also told him that if he continued to keep this thing to himself, it would eventually destroy him. He still didn't want to tell them, so I asked if he would let me tell his parents for him. I was relieved when he said I could, so with his permission, I went inside with him and told them about his secret. Then I stepped back and watched the three of them talk.

As I watched, there was much hugging and crying. He was no longer alone with his pain from the past. After a few minutes, I told them that I should leave and let them be a family without me being there, but they asked me to stay with them for a while longer. There were more tears and there was prayer – taking this hurt to our Heavenly Father.

Eventually, I left, relieved that this man was no longer alone with his pain. By the time I made it back to my place, the Super Bowl had already started. I tried to watch what was left of it, but I couldn't really focus on the game. It seemed so boring compared to watching our God at work that day.

We have a Heavenly Father who is a God of comfort and healing. On that Sunday evening, many of the homes around the world were filled with people watching the Super Bowl. But in one lone house on an obscure street in this one town there was a family huddled together, as God ministered to all of them, bringing His comfort and light to a man who needed a touch from God. He needed God's healing and the freedom from past hurts that only God can give – to help him as a husband, as a father and as a healthy, happy child of God. This man needed to know the message that God prompted me to say the night before: *"God sees him, he is not alone, God sees him as holy."*

As I write this, I'm reminded that the message above from God speaks to me too. God knows my past and He sees me as I am today – flawed. In spite of this, God loves me – I'm not alone. He sees me as holy, not because of who I am but because of who Jesus is and because I belong to Him. I am so blessed and so lucky because Jesus overlooks my faults and walks with me. He accepts me as I am. It's easy to walk forward to love others because it's His love I'm taking to the world. His presence and His power shines bright, as a light that overcomes any darkness . . . I'm not alone!!! You are not alone!!!

❦❦❦❦❦❦❦❦❦❦❦❦❦❦❦❦❦

God sees your past … He sees who you are today …
He has a wonderful plan for your future.
Do you have any regrets from the past? Any hurts?
Take them to God … He forgives and He comforts.

Chapter 32

Help

*Pure and genuine religion in the sight of God the Father
means caring for orphans and widows in their distress
and refusing to let the world corrupt you.*
James 1:27

The phone rang. It was my daughter Jennifer. She said, "Dad, Julie and I were in a store that we've never been in before. While we were there, I saw a friend I haven't seen in a long time. Dad, she needs help right away. She's 82 years old, she's a widow and she works part time at the store. She's living with her dog in a room she rents from a friend. Her friend took her rent for the month and then told her she has to move out."

"Dad, she has no place to go. She has a little money saved up but not enough to get into a new place. We have to help."

As I listened, my first response was to look at the situation logically. . . not with faith. I said, "OK, but I'd like to meet her first and hear more about her story. We'll try to help, but I don't know what we can do in one day. We don't have a lot of extra money, but I'm sure we can help a little. It's going to be hard for her to find a place that allows for her dog without wanting a large deposit."

Then my daughter reminded me, "Dad, the Bible says that true religion is helping widows and orphans. We have to help." *(James 1:27)*

Of course, she was right. Once again, my daughter was the teacher and I was the student. *True religion is not about going to church and following all the rules. It's about loving God and loving others as we do ourselves (Mark 12:29-31).* I hung up the phone and began praying about this need. I didn't know how God would answer, but I knew He would.

My, how quickly God put together a team of people to help! My good friend, Julie, invited this woman and her dog to stay with her and her family – rent free. Then, we made a few calls and sent out an e-mail explaining the need.

As soon as possible, I met with the woman so I could find out more about the situation. I expected to find someone who was very frail and timid and scared by her current situation. But to my surprise, I found someone who was strong and happy and optimistic. She was a delightful person to talk with.

For several weeks there was no response to our e-mail or calls. Then, one Saturday morning, I was meeting with my friend, Marcus, to read the Bible together, and my phone rang. It was a friend of mine who had just been given a lot of very nice used furniture. He said he would bring it over for our friend to use once she found a place of her own. I was excited about the furniture, so when I hung up, I told Marcus briefly about what was happening. He asked me a few questions about the woman in need and then said he would pay for all her costs to move into a new place. So, within a few days, this sweet elderly woman was in her new home with her furniture and her dog.

Although a few people know about our friend getting help to move into a new home, very few know the complete story. They aren't aware that when Julie opened up her home to this lady and her dog – she did it joyfully, even though she was dealing with a number of very difficult issues. Or that my friend who called about the furniture had just recently suffered a devastating business setback (by the way – he is also the car wash guy mentioned in chapter 34). Marcus, wrote the check to cover the move-in expenses, without hesitation, although he had recently experienced a lot of unusually large personal expenses.

When God wants to send someone to help a person in

♠ A BURRO FOR JESUS

need – He doesn't always send people who are the most qualified or the most able – often He sends those who are most willing. He often sends the people who understand that God wants us to take our eyes off of ourselves and put them on Him and the needs of the people around us.

By the way, as I am writing this chapter, our friend has now been in her new home for about two weeks. I stopped by to see her yesterday. She's doing well and loves her new home. As we talked for a while, I couldn't help but think about how different things would be for her if God had not seen her situation and sent someone to help. I'm so glad He cares so much. I'm so glad He sent us.

What if she hadn't prayed and asked God to help her? What if Jennifer and Julie hadn't gone to that store (on the same day our friend was in danger of having nowhere to live)? What if Julie hadn't invited her to stay with her and her family? What if my friends hadn't donated everything needed for her to move into the new apartment?

What if God ignored people in need? Fortunately, He doesn't! He sees them and He hears their prayers. He gives His followers what is needed to take care of others. He allows us to choose how we use what we have. What if God's children obeyed His command to love our neighbors as ourselves and looked for ways to help others? What if our only goal is to glorify our Heavenly Father with our words, thoughts and actions? What if our obsession, our passion is Jesus – the wonderful Son of God?

✿✿✿✿✿✿✿✿✿✿✿✿✿✿✿✿

What if we loved people the way Jesus does?

What if . . .

Chapter 33

Breakfast Burritos and Bible

*Your word is a lamp to guide my feet
and a light for my path.*
Psalm 119:105

For years, it was my habit to go to a local restaurant on Sunday mornings to have about two hours with my coffee, my breakfast burrito and my Bible before attending the morning church service. It was my quiet time with God – to read and pray and enjoy His presence. **Have you ever noticed how the relationships with people you love are enriched when you spend quality time together?** Well, the same is true about our relationship with God. There is no substitute for having quiet time alone with Him. We learn to hear God better when we are alone with Him often.

One particular Sunday morning, I noticed a man who came to the same restaurant every week just like I did, at about the same time. He was a little older than me and he always sat a few tables away from where I usually sat. For weeks I would say hello to him, then go to my table to read. Then, one day while I was there praying, I thought about him. He and I were both there every week. It made perfect sense that we should become friends and for me to introduce him to Jesus, if he didn't already know Him. And if he did, we could enjoy time with Jesus, as we prayed and read the Bible together.

So, I walked over to his table. After we briefly intro-duced ourselves to each other, I said, "I noticed you and I come here every Sunday and we sit in the same area. I come here to read my Bible and pray. I was wondering if you'd like to join me each week for a little time in the Bible. You see, God has been the best part of my life for years and I love reading the Bible."

"No," he said, "I'd never want to do that. I don't want to read the Bible. That's not for me."

We talked for a moment longer then I tried again. I said, **"You know the Bible is one of the most popular, most published books of all time.** If we read it together, one of two things will happen. Either you will discover, as I did, that it contains God's words to us and your life will be changed forever. Or you won't discover that it's God's words, even though it is. Either way, we'll become friends and we'll each learn a little more about the best book ever written. Whatever happens, it will be time well spent."

"No," he insisted. "That's not for me."

"OK," I said. "Well, I'm glad we met. Have a great day." And I left for church.

When I got to the restaurant the following week, he was already there. I said hi to him and continued on to my table. When he finished eating he came over to me and said, "OK. What's the lesson for today?" I was both surprised and pleased that he had accepted my offer. So, I invited him to sit down and I shared a short devotional thought with him from the Bible.

This was the first of many Sundays when we met to read from God's word and talk briefly about what we had read. Some weeks he wanted to talk about current events, so we would look in the Bible for something that spoke to what was happening in the world at that time. He became a friend who I really enjoyed seeing every week.

Occasionally, one of his friends would join us. Then, I met two homeless guys there and they stopped by for Bible time every now and then. I invited a couple of other guys who were there every week also, but they didn't join us. In fact, one of them would always turn and walk away from me every time he saw me. Some weeks there were only two of us. Sometimes there were three or four of us. God was always with us – speaking to us through the Bible.

I looked forward to my Sunday mornings. I would have my personal time with God and my time reading the Bible with my new friends. For about a year we had our own "little church service" at the restaurant. I don't know how God will use that time together in the lives of all of us. I do know that any time we read the Bible (with others or alone), it is used by God to impact our lives.

🌾🌾🌾🌾🌾🌾🌾🌾🌾🌾🌾🌾🌾🌾🌾🌾

Have you enjoyed any time in the Bible today?
The day is not over . . . Open it up . . .
Enjoy it . . . Absorb it . . . Marinate in it.

It's one of God's special gifts to us . . .
It has answers for this life and the next.

Chapter 34

God Wants What God Wants

Seek His (God's) will in all you do, and
He will show you what path to take.
Proverbs 3:6

God knows what God wants. He wants us to discover His son Jesus. He wants us to follow Jesus and become like Him. He wants to rescue us from any path we are on that excludes Him and eventually leads to pain and disaster. He is patient. He doesn't want us to die before we discover who He is and what His plan is for us. **So, He pursues us with a passion that is only displayed by someone pursuing the one they love dearly.**

I remember times in the past when God used me as He pursued others. And I remember times when I was drifting down the wrong path and He pursued me to rescue me from my mistakes. One such time was when my wife and I both thought we were headed toward a divorce. We had been married for about 20 years. It was a busy, hectic time in our lives and we weren't communicating well with each other. We were still together but we weren't very happy together. We just couldn't seem to get along and we argued a lot. I thought it was all her fault and I blamed her.

Then, one day God got my attention. I was on our back patio and the thoughts I sensed from God were very direct: "Bert, this is your fault, not hers. You thought she would always be like the teenager you met . . . care-free, fun-loving, romantic, happy and focused solely on you. You've changed over the past 20 years. Now you're upset because she's changed too. Your thoughts are on what you want, not on what she wants. Stop being so selfish. This is not about what she can do for you. It's about what you can do for her. Love her the way I love you. Cherish her."

He was right. I had been wrong. So, I began changing the way I treated her and how I spoke to her. I tried to take my eyes off of myself and put them back onto her and her needs.

About the same time she came to me and said, "You know we've lost the love we used to have for each other. Let's pray and ask God to give it back to us again."

So, we prayed and He did just what we asked of Him. That was about 20 years ago and our love for each other and for Him continues to grow!!!!

God, thank You for rescuing my marriage. You showed me, over time, how much You value marriage. You designed it to be a union between the three of us – You, her and me . . . not just me and her. **Marriage is one of Your ways of showing the world a picture of the relationship we can have with You.** You overlook our faults and invite us to be Your "bride" – the object of Your eternal, selfless love. How wrong of us to think that marriage is about us and our needs. Marriage is not intended to complete us – You are. How sad it is that we are so willing to give up on marriage when it becomes hard. How beautiful marriage is when it is the three of us – with Your love and forgiveness flowing through us to our marriage partner. When our love for them resembles Your love for us – *when our love is patient, kind, not envious, not boastful, not proud, not conceited, not selfish, not easily angered, does not demand its own way, does not remember past wrongs, finds no joy in evil, rejoices in the truth . . . when it always protects, always trusts, always hopes, and endures all things . . . that* kind of love only comes from You (*1 Corinthians, chapter 13*).

That was one of the times when God pursued me and rescued me. Then there were the times when God let me be a part of His plan as He pursued other people . . . Like the guy I met who was working at the car wash. As he wrote the ticket for my car wash and walked away, something inside me prompted me to go after him to tell him about Jesus. After I caught up with him, I was a bit clumsy in my attempt to talk to him. In fact, at that moment when we were standing and facing each other, I couldn't think of anything at all to say. I knew I had to do something so I handed him the little Bible I carried in my pocket for times like this.

"I'm sorry to interrupt you," I said. "I know you're busy. But I want you to have this Bible. It's about my best friend Jesus. By the way, do you know Him?"

His answer surprised me. "I'm Jewish," he said.

"That's OK," I said. "So is He. Would you like to know more about Him?"

"Actually, I am interested in spiritual things. I would like to know more," he said.

I was surprised by his response and also delighted that he wanted to talk about Jesus. He said he was off every Monday and that I could call him on Sunday to schedule a time to meet for lunch on the following day. The next day was Sunday, so I called to see if we could set up a time to meet. He said he was too busy that week so I asked his permission to call him the following week. He said OK, but when I called him a week later he again said he was too busy. This went on for about 6 months. Each week I called and each week he said he was too busy and we would have to wait until the following week. I thought he might think it was a bit odd that I continued to call him every week so I told him repeatedly that I was not a weirdo. I told him that I really looked forward to telling him about my friend Jesus. Then, I would again ask for his permission for me to call him the following week.

This went on and on until finally one week he agreed to meet for lunch. So, we met and had a really good conversation about God and about Jesus being the Messiah promised in the Bible. We met often for several months and he asked a lot of good questions about God. He was sincerely searching for answers about God and about life. As expected, the Bible gave him the answers he was looking for and over time, he accepted the truth about Jesus being his Messiah and he decided to give his heart and his life to Jesus.

He told me later that the only reason he met with me was because of a girl that he had been talking to online for months. He told her about the guy who gave him a Bible at the car wash and then called him every week to meet. She was a Christian and she made him promise her that he would stop putting me off. He promised her that he would agree to meet with me the next time I called him. So, that's why we met. Wow! When God pursues someone, He really does it right!

It's now about fifteen years later and he and I are still good friends. After he became a Christian, we continued to meet as often as we could to talk about spiritual matters. Then, within a few years after his decision to follow Jesus, he asked if I would meet with him and a few of his friends every week. They had started to meet to read a book about God, but some of them were not Christians and they had questions about what they were reading. He thought I could be of help by becoming a part of their conversations about God.

I told him that I'd love to meet with them but since I was a newly invited guest to their group, I'd sit in the back of the room and take a passive role in their discussion, unless there was a question directed my way. It seemed more appropriate to me that I not say a lot at first until we all got to know each other better.

I still remember when I walked into the room to meet with them for the first time. Before I could quietly slip into a seat in the back, one of the women said, "So you're Bert. What's all this stuff about Jesus and why is it so important to have Him in my life?"

So much for quietly joining the group and slowly joining their conversations! I was a bit surprised by her direct questions, but I really liked her honesty. It was refreshing to meet someone who said exactly what she was thinking. I briefly answered her questions and sat down. My first meeting with them had begun. For about a year we met weekly to talk about the book and about the things of God. We became friends quickly and I really looked forward to seeing them every week.

After we finished the book, we took a break for a while. Then, a year or so later, we decided to start meeting again to study a second book. I have such good memories of them and all the conversations we had about God as well as other things. I was and am so blessed to know them. I don't see them as often now. When my wife and I recently moved to a new town, many of them showed up to surprise me at a Bible study/prayer group I was leading, even though I hadn't seen most of them in years. It was one of the highlights of the evening for me.

Then there was the time when I was at the airport several hours before my flight was to leave. I asked God to give me someone there to talk to who was in need of Him. The first guy I talked to was not interested at all in talking about Jesus, so I changed the subject. Although my initial conversation with him was casual and non-threatening, he still didn't want to talk about spiritual matters. That's unfortunate but it happens. **It's important when we invite people to take a look at Jesus – that we do it in a gentle, respectful way, and also listen to them and their stories … not just "preach" at them.**

After the first guy walked away to go to his flight, someone else sat down by me. We talked about various things for a while, then he told me about some of the difficulties in his life. For about 30 minutes we took a wonderful journey through the Bible – looking at the promises God makes to all who believe.

It was a special time set up by God. A day or so after I got home, he called me to thank me for our conversation. He said he had shared the Bible verses with his wife that he and I had read together. They had both been blessed by their time together in the Bible and had decided to start going to church again.

It's so easy for any of us to get off the right path to chase after something we think we want – only to find that we are on the wrong path. That happened to me for a while and my marriage suffered because of it. Then, God pursued me, caught me and showed me a better way. Now, He uses me (when I let Him) as He pursues others.

God sees you. He wants the best for you. He has a path for you that is in your best interest and glorifies Him. Have you been running in the wrong direction – away from God? Are you tired of chasing things that will never completely satisfy you? I've got a good idea. Stop running away. Turn to God. His ways are so much better than our ways. His thoughts are so much better than our thoughts. Stop settling for second best. God's way, through Jesus is better. God wants you to enjoy a fulfilling, joyful life.

꧁꧂꧁꧂꧁꧂꧁꧂꧁꧂꧁꧂꧁

God wants what He wants . . . He wants you . . . Go to Him!

Chapter 35

Our Children

Train up a child in the way he should go, and when he is old he will not depart from it.
Proverbs 22:6 (NKJ)

I have three children. They are such a joy to me. They were all raised to follow Jesus. They are all really great kids, but as they reached their teens, they became busy with life and were exposed to ideas different than the ones they heard from their Mom and me. Over time, they began to pursue other interests and seemed to loose their desire for a close relationship with God. It broke my heart. I desperately wanted God to bring them all back to Himself.

Although I looked for opportunities to talk to them and help them find their way back to God, it became obvious that my prayers for them would probably accomplish more than my words to them. So I prayed for them often. At first, my prayers were asking God to help them fall completely and passionately in love with Him. But, over time, my prayers changed. I asked Him to do whatever He had to do to get their attention. I asked Him to bring them to their knees, if He had to, so they would turn their eyes and hearts back to Him.

I'm sure I will always remember the conversation I had one day with my daughter, Jennifer. We were headed to Colorado for a few days to see our friend Kelly get baptized. I had been concerned for a while about Jennifer's apparent lack of interest in the things of God. Knowing we would be together for several days on this trip, I had been asking God to set up an opportunity for me to have a meaningful talk with her about her relationship with Him. We had been on the road for less than an hour when

Jennifer brought up the subject.

She asked, "Do you remember when I stopped reading my Bible and I stopped listening to Christian music? Do you ever wonder why I stopped?" I told her I had thought about that a lot.

"Do you ever wonder why I don't want to go to church anymore?" I told her that I had thought about that a lot also.

She went on to tell me during this and subsequent conversations that she had decided to stop the typical religious activities – not because she was disinterested in God, but because she wanted a deeper walk with Him. At first this made no sense to me at all. She said that she saw kids her age who went to church but didn't take God seriously. She didn't want to be one of those people who acted one way at church and then acted differently the rest of the time.

She also knew people who had lived without God in their lives – then found a wonderful, exciting relationship with Him. She had never known a time when God was not a part of her life. Maybe if she walked away from Him for a while, she would find the same thing they did. So, she stopped all the outward visible practices of Christianity, thinking she would have a deeper love for God when she returned to Him. Although her logic still didn't make a lot of sense to me, it did to her and it was born out of her hunger for more of God – and that's always a good thing.

You know, the best thing we can do as parents is to help our children develop a true loving relationship with God. Nothing we do as parents will ever impact their lives more than that. As I had these discussions with my daughter, I realized there is an aspect to a child's walk with God that may not be obvious to us as they are growing up.

As I told Jennifer during one of our talks, "One of the problems with being raised in a Christian home and going to church since you were small is that you have always believed in God because your Mom and I told you He was real. We also told you that the Easter bunny and Santa Claus were real."

"You see." I continued. "If this thing with God is going to be meaningful to you, you have to find out who God is for yourself. You can't just believe in Him because we do. **I don't want you to be a casual Christian sitting in a pew and not ever having a real deep walk with God.** If you are ever going to play a meaningful role in God's kingdom, you have to ask Him the tough questions. He's a big boy. He can take it. He understands your doubts and He'll answer your questions. I want you to follow Him completely because you want to, not just play the game."

I want my children to be honest with God, to ask Him to answer their questions about Him. I want their faith to be real, not a set of religious practices that means very little to them.

If our faith in God is going to be sincere, it must be based on a true love for Him, not by participating in religious activities in a casual way. A loving relationship is built upon knowing someone so well that there is complete trust and honesty. It's not based on rules and regulations.

It's been years now since my children became disinterested in God. After years of praying, I now see them all walking with God through all the ups and downs of this life. God answered my prayers for my children. I so love God even more than before because He brought my children back to Himself. As it says in the Bible *(3 John, verse 4)* *"I have no greater joy than to hear that my children are following the truth."*

If you are a Christian parent . . . Pray often for your children . . . And walk the walk with Jesus in a way that honors Him. Your kids are watching. They need to hear about Jesus from you. But more than that, they need to see Him in you. If you're a Christian and are casual about this whole thing . . . Please remember that Jesus wasn't casual when He walked to the cross for you.

If you're not going to try to follow Him well – please don't tell people you are a follower of Jesus. They may form their opinion of Him by watching you. You're doing harm to God's efforts to bring people into His kingdom. There are lives at stake. May I suggest ... get on board completely with Him or walk away completely and get out of the way. Jesus told the people of the church, "I want you to be either hot for me or cold for me . . . never lukewarm" *(Revelation 3:15-16).*

᭟᭟᭟᭟᭟᭟᭟᭟᭟᭟᭟᭟᭟᭟᭟᭟᭟᭟

Dear reader – of the two, I hope you choose to be hot for Him (to get completely on board with Him). He's inviting you to follow Him and walk closely with Him. You'll never regret it.

Closing thoughts from a Burro

Chapter 36

Adventures

*For this is how God loved the world: He gave His
one and only Son, so that everyone who believes in Him
will not perish but have eternal life.*
John 3:16

Dear reader,

Thank you for joining me as I've told you about some of
my adventures with God. There have been more adventures over
the years, as I have devoted my life to following Him, but these are
the ones I wanted to include in this book. It's exciting to know that
there will be more adventures in the future because God continues
to work through anyone whose heart is truly committed to Him.
And I plan to stay truly committed to Him. I belong to Him for
His use (His burro).

How about you? Have you begun your adventure with
God yet?

If not, wouldn't you like to start today?

He wants you to know that He loves you dearly. He
knows everything about you –even the things you don't want anyone else to know about yourself. In spite of the things in your life
that God dislikes, He loves you dearly. He has a wonderful plan for
your life.

**God created you to have a close relationship with
Him.** He wants you to know Him personally and for you to
experience a life with true freedom – a life full of joy and meaning. He wants to lavish His love upon you, as any good father
wants to do for his child. When He created you, He allowed you

to decide what you would love most during your life. He wants you to love Him more than anything else. But He doesn't force you to love Him. True love is a choice, it is not forced. If you haven't yet begun your adventure with God, that means you have decided to love yourself more than Him. You have decided to pursue the things you want more than the things He wants for you.

The decisions you've made to exclude Him and do things that don't please Him . . . as you live to satisfy your own desires – God calls those things sin. That sin has created a gap between you and God, preventing you from experiencing the joy and contentment of living a life close to God and also preventing you from going to Heaven one day. God says that the penalty for sin is death – both physical death and spiritual death (being separated from God for all of eternity after this physical life ends). God also says that these sins can only be erased by a blood sacrifice.

Because of your sin, there is no way you can please God with your own efforts. You can't earn your way into His family. You can't earn your way into Heaven. God wants you in his family, as an heir to all His blessings. He wants you in Heaven with Him. So, God provided a way for you – through His son Jesus. He sent Jesus to Earth to live among us. Jesus told us, with His words and actions, about His Heavenly Father's love for us.

Then Jesus allowed Himself to be executed on a cross, shedding His blood as the sacrifice required by God for your sins and mine. He did this because God asked Him to ... so you and I can join Him in Heaven one day. That's how much God loves us. But the story doesn't end there. Three days later Jesus was raised from the dead to prove He was God and that death and sin had been defeated for all time.

Good News!! We couldn't get to God – so He came to us!
God invites you to turn from a life of living only for

yourself – a life that will never truly be fulfilling and turn to Him. If you have been living to satisfy your own desires and exclude God from your life . . . I ask you – how has that been working for you so far? God has a better life for you – a life that revolves around Him and His perfect plan for your life.

God asks you to believe in Him and His son Jesus. He invites you to accept Jesus' death on the cross as the sacrifice for your sin. He invites you to receive His son Jesus as the Lord of your life (to lead you through life). When you make this decision and ask God to forgive you for your disobedience, He forgives your sins and you become a part of His family – both now and for all of eternity. You can now know God personally.

You don't have to try to fix things in your life before you turn to Him. Simply turn away from your old life of living for yourself and turn to Him. We don't earn God's forgiveness by any good deeds we do. We receive this free gift from God (forgiveness of our sins and eternal life with Him) as a result of what Jesus did for us on the cross.

Your adventure with God begins when you repent of your past mistakes and turn to God. Then, as your new life of meaning and purpose continues, God will help you get to know Him on a deeper level. He'll continue the good work He has begun in you. He promises all of this in the Bible and He never breaks His promise.

To discover more about how to start your adventure with God, google – salvation through Jesus. You'll find several websites that explain this great gift that God is offering to you and how you can accept it. When you make the decision to devote your life to Jesus and follow Him, tell someone who you know has already become a true follower of Jesus about the decision you made. Ask them to read the Bible with you and to help you find a good Bible-teaching church.

If you are reading this and are still hesitating to receive

this new life that God is offering to you – I plead with you . . . turn to Jesus and be reconciled to God.

GOD HIMSELF is inviting you to become a part of His family, to become an heir to all that He has for you.

On a personal note, I decided to follow Jesus many years ago. I had no idea at that time how He would fill my life with purpose and joy. I had no idea that the things that were once important to me would fade in value compared to the joy of knowing Jesus – the one and only son of God who invited me to walk through life with Him . . .WOW - what an adventure it has been and continues to be . . . what a privilege to follow Him.

He gave me a new life . . . He'll do the same for you . . .

🌱🌱🌱🌱🌱🌱🌱🌱🌱🌱🌱🌱🌱🌱🌱

And this is what God has testified: He has given us eternal life, and this life is in His Son. Whoever has the Son has life; whoever does not have God's Son does not have life. I have written this to you who believe in the name of the Son of God, so that you may know you have eternal life. 1 John 5:11-13

Chapter 37

How About You?

So we don't look at the troubles we can see now;
rather, we fix our gaze on things that cannot be seen.
For the things we see now will soon be gone,
but the things we cannot see will last forever.
2 Corinthians 4:18

Do you hurt for the lost?
        ...for the sad and the lonely?
                ...for the downcast and the discouraged?

God does . . . *He is close to the brokenhearted and He rescues those whose spirits are crushed (Psalm 34:18).*

I have an idea . . . **Go to a cemetery and look at the names on the tombstones.** Of all the people buried there . . . Who do you think was the richest? Or the most popular? Or the most educated?

Who knows? And who really cares now? You see – most of the things they worked so hard to achieve in their earthly pursuits don't matter much now. The Bible teaches us that even though their physical bodies died, their spirits are still alive – either living with God for all of eternity or completely separated from God and all of His goodness for all of eternity.

That leads to the obvious question – are you and I living our lives for things that have eternal value or for things that have earthly value? **Jesus tells us in the Bible** *(Luke 12:15, 21)* **that life is not measured by how much we own.** He says that a person is a fool to store up worldly wealth but not have a rich relationship with God. He wants us to be focused on things that have eternal value. He wants to use us to help other people do the same. He wants you and I to offer His peace and salvation to people who are hurting, those who are lost.

We are all gifted in different ways. How God uses you to minister to others may be different than how He uses me. That's up to Him. But we are all called to love others and invite people to take a look at Jesus and the new life He offers to everyone. We are all called to encourage people (with our actions, our speech and our written words) to follow Jesus and let Him lead them through life.

You don't have to quit your job and move to a foreign country to be used by God (unless He asks you to). Just be faithful where you are . . . be obedient.

We are to do what God commands, not just read about it and then ignore it. As we thirst for God, His love flows out of us, to others with power. We are to be filled with the Holy Spirit (guided and led by the Holy Spirit). To have knowledge, skill or even faith and power, without the love of God, is to be ineffective for Kingdom purposes. *
*Paraphrased summary of James 1:22, John 7:37 - 38, Acts 1:8, Ephesians 5:18, Galatians 5:16, 5:25, 1 Corinthians 13:1-7

Are you ready to be a burro for Jesus? Think about a burro for a minute. Burros are used for important jobs because they are dependable. They are often used by their owners (masters) to carry valuable cargo to its destination. God wants to use us to carry His love (His precious cargo) to its destination – to the hearts and lives of the people around us.

How do you become a burro for Jesus?
There are some suggestions, on the next page . . .

Believe in Jesus . . . love Him and follow Him with passion.
Be obsessed with Him. Hunger and thirst for Him.

Understand the gospel message is not only for you – it's for
everyone. Don't keep it to yourself. People are living and
dying without Jesus.

Repent of your sins. Pray and ask for forgiveness.
Examine your heart and your motives.

Rest in God's presence and stay **R**ooted in His word.

Obey Him. Why read about God's power and majesty in the
Bible and then decide to not obey Him?
That doesn't make sense.

Submit to the leading of the Holy Spirit in every aspect of
your life. We receive the gift of the Holy Spirit when we
receive Jesus into our lives. But too many believers don't
invite the sweet presence of the Holy Spirit to dominate
their thoughts, their actions and their words daily. Bible
study is a very good thing, in fact, it's essential as a follower
of Jesus. But we are to seek more than academic pursuits, we
are to seek the daily leading of the Holy Spirit.

Jesus has burros all around the world.

Are you one of them?   If so – that's great – continue!

If not – why not?   What are you waiting for?

Message from the Author

Now that I am old and gray, do not abandon me, O God.
Let me proclaim Your power to this new generation,
Your mighty miracles to all who come after me.
Psalm 71:18

There was a time when I read about the heroes in the Bible and famous missionaries . . . and wished I could see God work the way they did. I wanted to see God's power. I wanted to see miracles.

Then God took me on the journey described in this book. He showed me that this walk with Him is not about His power and His miracles. It's about His love. It's not about trying to produce results to gain His favor. It's about our love affair with God. As we thirst and hunger for Him, He fills us to overflowing with His love. His love then touches lives through us... as we allow Him to use us for His purposes.

God is all-powerful and still does miracles. He's God. I've seen His power... I've seen His miracles. I've seen Him answer prayers . . . and I marvel. I marvel more at His love for us – that is so undeserved, but so obvious.

God's ultimate demonstration of His love is displayed through Jesus and His sacrifice on the cross – so that you and I can have our sins forgiven and become a part of God's Kingdom . . . now and forever!

Let me tell you about my Lord and best friend Jesus. He is alive and active in the world today. He is the single most influential man to ever walk on earth. He is the son of God, sent by God to live among us and to bring God's love and peace to your life and mine. Jesus is the only way to God. Jesus is God's light in a dark world. Jesus is truth. Jesus is life – abundant and everlasting. Jesus is love. We would need all the books ever written and more to tell all there is to know about Jesus. As I become older and my health is beginning to decline a little, I see each day as a gift from God . . . another day to live with Him and for Him.

❀❀❀❀❀❀❀❀❀❀❀❀❀❀❀❀❀

Jesus is the love of my life.

He asks me to follow Him . . . so I do.

Will you do the same?

Final Thoughts

Have you ever...

> **...wanted to hear from God but didn't hear anything at that moment?**

> **... tried to love someone and point them to Jesus and wonder if it helped at all, as you watched their actions?**

> **... wanted to do more for God and didn't know what to do?**

I have!

I had a talk with God a few months ago. I was feeling frustrated. I was disappointed and saddened by several formerly homeless people who we had recently helped. All of them were making bad decisions and it appeared our efforts were having very little positive effect at all.

"God, if you'd asked me which of your ministries I'd like to be a part of, I wouldn't have picked this one (ministry to the homeless). So, would you reconsider and reassign me to something different, something easier? I don't like this one right now."

I was having my own little pity party. **I'd temporarily forgotten that God asks us to love people, not fix them.** He's responsible for the results. He changes hearts and transforms lives, not us.

Fortunately, my feelings of self-pity were only momentary. I've known God long enough to know that His way is better than my way. He's known me long enough to know that my moment of frustration would be followed by my turning to Him and returning to the path we were walking together. I continue to obey Him because I love Him and I want to please Him. I'd rather be with Him, as He leads me to a place that may sometimes be difficult, than to stay where I'm at without Him.

Over the years I've read more than a few books on prayer, on discipleship and on ministry. I enjoyed them, but … I sometimes came away feeling like I had to do more … I had to get to a deeper place with God quickly … I wasn't getting it like others were…I wasn't being spiritual enough … I wasn't doing enough.

"I" … "I" … "I" … I think I see part of my problem, maybe yours too. It's the "I" thing that we struggle with our entire lives. It's what we've always been taught … if we want to accomplish more – we must set goals, make a plan and do more. That's the world's way. And it often leads to worldly success (as well as stress, worry, addictions, and broken lives).

It's not God's way. His way starts with Him, not us. The power comes from Him, not us. It's not our plan that counts, it's His plan and it's revealed to us through His Bible and through the daily leading of the Holy Spirit. His way may not make a lot of sense to some people. Just like it doesn't make a lot of sense that God loves us so much and wants to give us a new life, a new purpose and a new identity.

So…How do you and I learn to hear God better? How do we joyfully minister to others when circumstances are hard?

I'm not a theologian, but here's my answer …

Remember that time when you fell madly, head-over-heels in love with that guy or that girl? You obsessed about them. You dreamed about them. You wrote their name on anything you can find, including your own skin. You wanted to be with them all the time. You could sit with them for hours and neither of you had to say anything, because you were happy just being together. Or you would sit and stare at them from across the room. You studied them. You wanted to know everything about them.

You were in love and life was good! You did things for them just because you wanted to please them. Things were natural and easy. All the other things that once seemed important now paled in comparison to the one you loved. You delighted in them and they delighted in you. There was joy – unspeakable joy. You were in love with them … and they were in love with you!

Jesus already loves us like that. Really! When we begin to love Him like that and we spend a lot of time with Him, just because we want to … then we begin to hear Him more clearly and the ways in which we serve Him become a joy. They are no longer a task, no longer a chore, no longer a ministry. We may get tired but never burned out. We may get off tract but our hunger for Him and desire to follow Him brings us back on track. His overwhelming compassion for the lost and the hurting will begin to overwhelm us, too.

This walk with God is not about doing more and more for Him. It's about doing less in our own power and letting Him work through us, in His timing. **It's about our love affair with Him and His love affair with us.** Listen to what Jesus said to the church in Ephesus *(Revelation 2:2,4, NAS)* " *I know your deeds and your toil and your perseverance… But this I have against you, that you have left your first love."*

When we fall madly in love with Jesus, we begin to fall out of love with the things that displease Him. We must run from the other things in your life that don't please Him. Ask Him to help you do that. Ask others to help. **You can't love someone completely and expect that love to flourish while flirting with things that dishonor the one you love.**

His love can't be contained! As we surrender ourselves

to Him, He accomplishes more than we would ever expect – in our lives and in the lives of the people we minister to. Jesus talked about this in a wonderful section of the Bible – chapter 15 of John-that includes verse 5...*Jesus said, "I am the vine, and you are the branches, he who abides in Me and I in him, he bears much fruit, for apart from Me you can do nothing."*

🌿🌿🌿🌿🌿🌿🌿🌿🌿🌿🌿🌿🌿🌿🌿

Do you want to experience more of God in your life and see Him working through you as He builds His Kingdom?

Slow down ... open your Bible ... enjoy your time in the Word ... pray ... abide with Him ...fall madly in love with Jesus ...enjoy your journey with Him ...

Enjoy Jesus today!

Thank You

Jesus
As I conclude this book, I owe a very big THANK YOU to YOU. This joyful life I enjoy is only possible because of You and Your sacrifice for all of us. You are the reason I wake up every day with a smile. You are the reason I look forward to what You and I are going to do every day. . . I belong to You.

Stephanie
My wife and partner for life . . . God's best gift to me (after Jesus and the Holy Spirit). You and I have been on this journey together with Jesus for most of our lives - through easy times and hard times. Look at you - you are a precious jewel.

Jennifer
My daughter and partner in ministry. What a blessing you are. I have learned so much about our God from you.

Diana, Josh, Julie, Kelly
My "spiritual kids". You make me proud and you bring me joy.

Kelly
Thank you for drawing the burro used in this book.

Jay, Rose, Harold, Kathy
You ministered in Mexico before I joined you and you continued to do so after I left that ministry. You have been used by God to bless me and so many others as you love and serve our wonderful Lord.

Rick, Gary, Kathy, Tom
What can I say about how much I see Jesus in you. Thank you.

Thank You

The Encounter Group
Wow! I've never been a part of a group like you before – your love for Jesus and His Word; your love for each other and your desire to obey God has always been authentic and meaningful. Keep on keeping' on for Jesus.

Kathy, Wayne, Jim, Rob, Megan, Danny, Henry, Dan, Justin, Brad, Tom, Santiago, Caleb, John, Mark, Donna, Carlos, Sue, Gregorio, Derrick, Blanca, Faye, Furman, Kyoko, Stan, Michael, Rick, Norm, Scott, Jerry, James, Kristy, Stephen, Kelley & others
The journey is not over and the work is not over. Let's keep going with our Lord and His message of love. To "Muppet Man", "Easy", "Fanta", "Iceman", "Tamale", "Tarbaby" - great nicknames you picked up in Mexico. You came to Mexico to serve God with us, and four of you fell in love with those four girls in our group . . . then you married them . . .Way to go !!!!!!!!!
You got more than you ever expected.

Jesus
I adore You. You are the same yesterday, today and forever. You are the beginning, the middle and the end. I began this book by thanking You and I end the same way...**THANK YOU!!!**

❦❦❦❦❦❦❦❦❦❦❦❦❦❦❦❦

Jesus is the same yesterday, today and forever.
He is worthy to be praised!

The disciples went and did as Jesus had instructed them. They brought the donkey and the colt and placed their cloaks on them for Jesus to sit on. A very large crowd spread their cloaks on the road, while others cut branches from the trees and spread them on the road. The crowds that went ahead of him and those that followed shouted,

"Hosanna to the Son of David!"
"Blessed is he who comes in the name of the Lord!"

This took place to fulfill what was spoken through the prophet:

"Say to Daughter Zion, 'See, your king comes to you,
gentle and riding on a donkey, and on a colt, the foal of a donkey.'"
Matthew 21:4-9

Now all glory to God, who is able, through His mighty power at work within us, to accomplish infinitely more than we might ask or think. Glory to Him in the church and in Christ Jesus through all generations forever and ever!

Ephesians 3:20

Made in the USA
Columbia, SC
29 January 2018